Graph-Based Methods for Natural Language Processing Workshop 2014

(TextGraphs-9)

Held at the Conference on Empirical Methods in Natural Language Processing (EMNLP 2014)

Doha, Qatar
29 October 2014

ISBN: 978-1-63439-480-2

Printed from e-media with permission by:

Curran Associates, Inc.
57 Morehouse Lane
Red Hook, NY 12571

CURRAN ASSOCIATES INC. proceedings.com

Some format issues inherent in the e-media version may also appear in this print version.

Printed by Curran Associates, Inc. (2014)

Association for Computational Linguistics
209 N. Eighth Street
Stroudsburg, Pennsylvania 18360

Phone: 1-570-476-8006
Fax: 1-570-476-0860

acl@aclweb.org

Additional copies of this publication are available from:

Curran Associates, Inc.
57 Morehouse Lane
Red Hook, NY 12571 USA
Phone: 845-758-0400
Fax: 845-758-2634
Email: curran@proceedings.com
Web: www.proceedings.com

TextGraphs-9

Graph-Based Methods for Natural Language Processing

Proceedings of the Workshop

October 29, 2014
Doha, Qatar

Production and Manufacturing by
Taberg Media Group AB
Box 94, 562 02 Taberg
Sweden

Introduction to TextGraphs-9

Welcome to TextGraphs, the workshop on Graph-based Methods for Natural Language Processing. The ninth edition of the workshop is being organized on October 29, 2014, in conjunction with the Conference on Empirical Methods in Natural Language Processing (EMNLP), 2014 in Doha, Qatar.

For the past eight years, the series of TextGraphs workshops have exposed and encouraged the synergy between the field of Graph Theory and Natural Language Processing (NLP). The mix between the two started small, with graph theoretical framework providing efficient and elegant solutions for NLP applications that focused on single documents for part-of-speech tagging, word sense disambiguation and semantic role labelling, got progressively larger with ontology learning and information extraction from large text collections, and have reached web scale through the new fields of research that focus on information propagation in social networks, rumor proliferation, e-reputation, multiple entity detection, language dynamics learning and future events prediction to name but a few.

The ninth edition of the TextGraphs workshop would be a new step in the series, focused on issues and solutions for large-scale graphs, such as those derived for web-scale knowledge acquisition or social networks. We encourage the description of novel NLP problems or applications that have emerged in recent years which can be addressed with graph-based solutions, as well as novel graph-based methods that can be applied to known NLP tasks. Continuing to bring together researchers interested in Graph Theory applied to Natural Language Processing provides an environment for further integration of graph-based solutions into NLP tasks. A deeper understanding of new theories of graph-based algorithms is likely to help create new approaches and widen the usage of graphs for NLP applications.

This volume contains papers accepted for presentation at the workshop. We issued calls for regular papers, short papers, position papers, and demos. After careful review by the program committee, 6 regular papers and 2 short papers were accepted for presentation. The accepted papers address varied problems – from theoretical and general considerations, to NLP and real-world applications - through interesting variations to known and also novel graph-based methods.

We are lucky to have two excellent invited speakers for this year's event. We thank Prof. Mohammed J. Zaki and Partha Talukdar for their enthusiastic acceptance to our invitation.

Finally, we are thankful to the members of the program committee for their valuable and high quality reviews. All submissions have benefited from their expert feedback. Their timely contribution was the basis for accepting an excellent list of papers and making this edition of TextGraphs a success.

V.G.Vinod Vydiswaran, Amarnag Subramanya, Gabor Melli, and Irina Matveeva

October 2014

Workshop Organizers:

V.G.Vinod Vydiswaran, University of Michigan (USA)
Amarnag Subramanya, Google (USA)
Gabor Melli, VigLink (USA)
Irina Matveeva, NexLP (USA)

Program Committee:

Asif Ekbar, Indian Institute of Technology, Patna (India)
Filip Ginter, University of Turku (Finland)
Rada Mihalcea, University of Michigan (USA)
Animesh Mukherjee, Indian Institute of Technology, Kharagpur (India)
Philippe Muller, Paul Sabatier University (France)
Preslav Nakov, Qatar Computing Research Institute (Qatar)
Günter Neumann, DFKI, Saarbrücken (Germany)
Arzucan Özgür, Bogazici University (Turkey)
Simone Paolo Ponzetto, University of Mannheim (Germany)
Delip Rao, Twitter (USA)
Martin Riedl, Darmstadt University of Technology (Germany)
Fabio Massimo Zanzotto, University of Rome (Italy)

Invited Speakers:

Mohammed J. Zaki, Rensselaer Polytechnic Institute (USA)
Partha Talukdar, Indian Institute of Science (India)

Table of Contents

Conference Program

Wednesday, October 29, 2014

Session 1

09:00–09:10 *Welcome and Introduction*
The organizers

09:10–10:15 *Keynote Talk*
Prof. Mohammed J. Zaki

10:15–10:30 *Normalized Entity Graph for Computing Local Coherence*
Mohsen Mesgar and Michael Strube

10:30–11:00 ***Coffee break***

Session 2

11:00–11:25 *Exploiting Timegraphs in Temporal Relation Classification*
Natsuda Laokulrat, Makoto Miwa and Yoshimasa Tsuruoka

11:25–11:50 *Multi-document Summarization Using Bipartite Graphs*
Daraksha Parveen and Michael Strube

11:50–12:15 *A Novel Two-stage Framework for Extracting Opinionated Sentences from News Articles*
Pujari Rajkumar, Swara Desai, Niloy Ganguly and Pawan Goyal

12:15–12:30 *Constructing Coherent Event Hierarchies from News Stories*
Goran Glavaš and Jan Šnajder

12:30–14:00 ***Lunch***

Wednesday, October 29, 2014 (continued)

Session 3

14:00–15:05 *Invited Talk*
Prof. Partha Talukdar

15:05–15:30 *Semi-supervised Graph-based Genre Classification for Web Pages*
Noushin Rezapour Asheghi, Katja Markert and Serge Sharoff

15:30–16:00 ***Coffee break***

Session 4

16:00–16:25 *The Modular Community Structure of Linguistic Predication Networks*
Aaron Gerow and James Evans

16:25–16:50 *From Visualisation to Hypothesis Construction for Second Language Acquisition*
Shervin Malmasi and Mark Dras

16:50–17:00 *Conclusion*
The organizers

Normalized Entity Graph for Computing Local Coherence

Mohsen Mesgar and **Michael Strube**
Heidelberg Institute for Theoretical Studies gGmbH
Schloss-Wolfsbrunnenweg 35
69118 Heidelberg, Germany
(mohsen.mesgar|michael.strube)@h-its.org

Abstract

Guinaudeau and Strube (2013) introduce a graph based model to compute local entity coherence. We propose a computationally efficient normalization method for these graphs and then evaluate it on three tasks: sentence ordering, summary coherence rating and readability assessment. In all tasks normalization improves the results.

1 Introduction

Guinaudeau and Strube (2013) introduce a graph based model (henceforth called *entity graph*) to compute local entity coherence. Despite being unsupervised, the entity graph performs on par with Barzilay and Lapata's (2005; 2008) supervised entity grid on the tasks of sentence ordering, summary coherence rating and readability assessment. The entity graph also overcomes shortcomings of the entity grid with regard to computational complexity, data sparsity and domain dependence.

The entity graph is a bipartite graph where one set of nodes represents entities and the other set of nodes represents the sentences of a document. Guinaudeau and Strube (2013) apply a one mode projection on sentence nodes (Newman, 2010) and then compute the average out-degree of sentence nodes to determine how coherent a document is. They describe variants of their entity graph which take the number of shared entities between sentences and their grammatical functions into account thus resulting in weighted bipartite graphs and weighted one mode projections. Here, we propose to normalize weights for the entity graph. Normalization allows to include distance between mentions of the same entity, which improves the performance on all three tasks thus confirming research in related areas which states that normalizing weights leads to better performance (Zhou et al., 2008; Zweig and Kaufmann, 2011).

2 The Entity Graph

The entity graph (Guinaudeau and Strube, 2013), $G = (V, E)$, represents the relations between sentences and entities in a text, where node set V contains all sentences and entities in a text and E is the set of all edges between sentences and entities. Let function $w(s_i, e_j)$ indicate the weight of an edge which connects sentence s_i and entity e_j. If $w(s_i, e_j) = 1$, then this edge indicates that there is a mention of e_j in sentence s_i. In order to realize the insight from Grosz et al. (1995) that certain syntactic roles are more important than others, the syntactic role of e_j in s_i can be mapped to an integer value (Guinaudeau and Strube, 2013):

$$w(s_i, e_j) = \begin{cases} 3 & \text{if } e_j \text{ is subject in } s_i \\ 2 & \text{if } e_j \text{ is object in } s_i \\ 1 & \text{otherwise} \end{cases}$$

Figure 1 illustrates a weighted entity graph for three sentences.

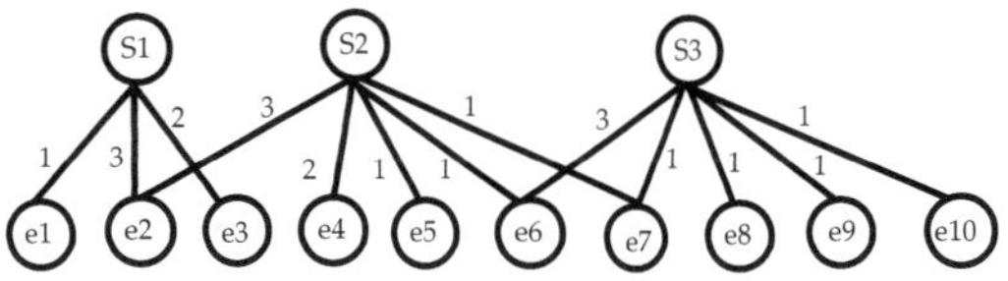

Figure 1: Weighted entity graph

Three types of one-mode projections capture relations between sentences, P_U, P_W and P_{Acc}. P_U creates an edge between two sentences if they share at least one entity. P_W captures the intuition that the connection between two sentences is stronger the more entities they share by means of weighted edges, where the weights equal the number of entities shared by sentences (Newman, 2004). The third type of projection, P_{Acc}, integrates syntactic information in the edge weights calculated by the following formula:

$$W_{ik} = \sum_{e \in E_{ik}} w(e, s_i) \cdot w(e, s_k) \, .$$

Figure 2 shows the three kinds of one-mode projections used in the entity graph.

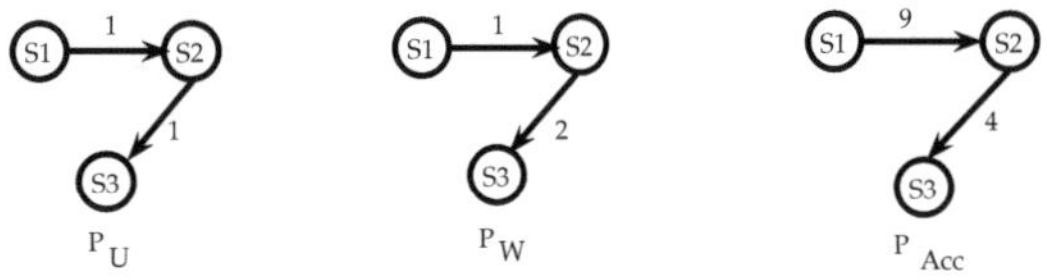

Figure 2: One-mode projections

While the entity grid (Barzilay and Lapata, 2008) uses information about sentences which do not share entities by means of the "- -" transition, the entity graph cannot employ this negative information. Here, we propose a normalization for the entity graph and its corresponding one-mode projections which is based on the *relative* importance of entities and, in turn, the *relative* importance of sentences. Including negative information allows to normalize the importance of entities according to sentence length (measured in terms of entity mentions), and hence to capture distance information between mentions of the same entity. This brings the entity graph closer to Stoddard's (1991, p.30) notion of cohesion: "The relative cohesiveness of a text depends on the number of cohesive ties [...] and on the distance between the nodes and their associated cohesive elements." By using this information, edge weights are set less arbitrary which leads to the more sound method and higher performance in all tasks.

3 Normalized Entity Graph

The entity graph weighs edges by the number of entities sentences share (P_W) and which syntactic functions the entities occupy (P_{Acc}). Here we normalize the weights by the number of entities in a sentence. This takes negative information into account as entities which do not occur in other sentences also count. Hence normalization captures the relative importance of entities as well as the relative importance of sentences.

We follow Newman (2004) by applying node degree normalization. For P_W, we divide the weight of each edge by the degree of the corresponding sentence node. If a sentence contains many entities, then the amount of information each entity contributes is reduced. Assume $\|s_i\|$ as the number of entities in sentence s_i. The importance of entity e_j for s_i is

$$Imp(s_i, e_j) = \frac{1}{\|s_i\|} .$$

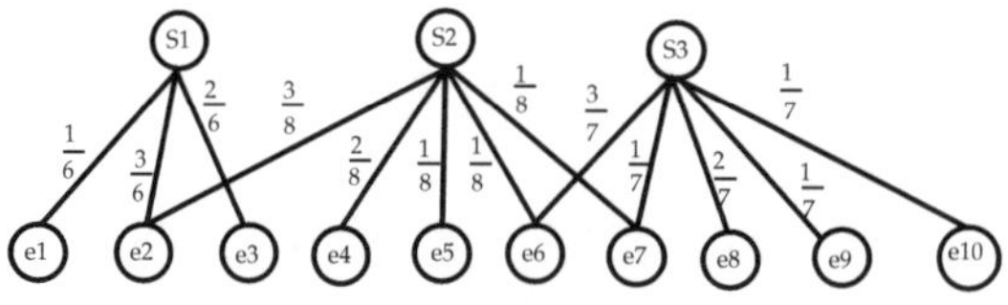

Figure 3: Normalized entity graph

For P_{Acc} we divide the weight of each edge by the sum of all edges' weights of a sentence. This gives the importance of each entity in a sentence relative to the sentence's other entities (see Figure 3).

$$Imp(s_i, e_j) = \frac{w(s_i, e_j)}{\sum_{e_e \in Entities} w(s_i, e_e)} .$$

For also normalizing the one-mode projection we introduce a virtual node TC capturing the textual content of all sentences (inspired by the graph based information retrieval model of Rode (2008)). The virtual node TC is connected to all sentences (see Figure 4).

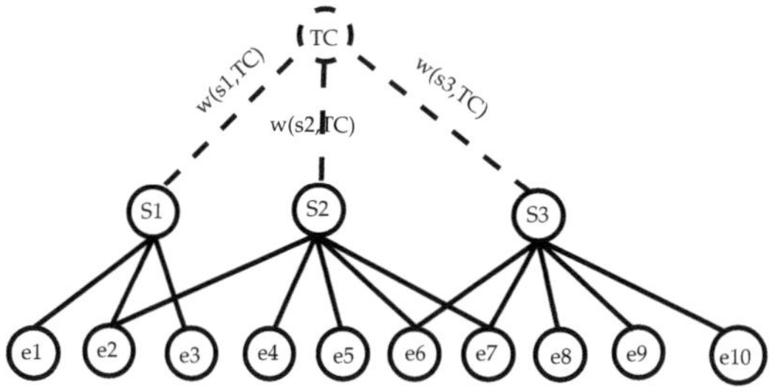

Figure 4: Entity graph with virtual node

Rode (2008) uses the following formula to compute weights on the edges between the sentence nodes and TC:

$$w(s_i, TC) = \frac{Score(s_i|TC)}{\sum_{s_t} Score(s_t|TC)} ,$$

where the function $Score(s_i|TC)$ is the number of entities in s_i which have overlap with TC. This value is equal to the degree of each sentence.

Since we are interested in local coherence, we restrict TC to pairs of sentences (See Figure 5). Subsequently, instead of $w(s_i, TC)$, we use the notation $lw_{s_i}^{s_j}$ (local weight of sentence s_i according to sentence s_j).

We define the normalized one-mode projection as follows:

$$W_{s_{ij}} = \sum_{e \in E_{s_{ij}}} \left\{ (lw_{s_i}^{s_j} \cdot Imp(s_i, e)) + (lw_{s_j}^{s_i} \cdot Imp(s_j, e)) \right\} .$$

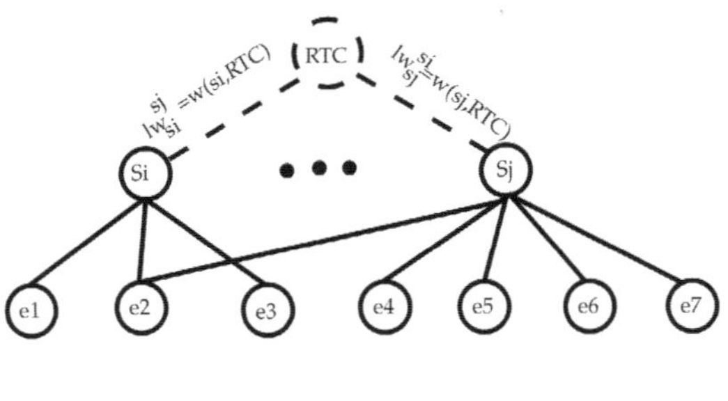

Figure 5: Restricted TC for a pair of sentences

Similar to Rode (2008), we use the product of $lw_{s_i}^{s_j}$ and $Imp(s_i, e)$ to approximate the salience of entity e in sentence s_i. This prevents the model to get biased by the length of sentences.

This method can be applied to graphs with edges weighted according to syntactic role (P_{Acc}). To compute the connection's strength of a pair of sentences we follow Yang and Knoke's (2001) approach: The path length in a weighted graph is the sum of the edge weights in the path. In our case, each path is defined between a pair of sentences of the entity graph, so the number of edges of all paths are equal to two. Figure 6 shows the normalized projections where the weights have been computed by the above formula.

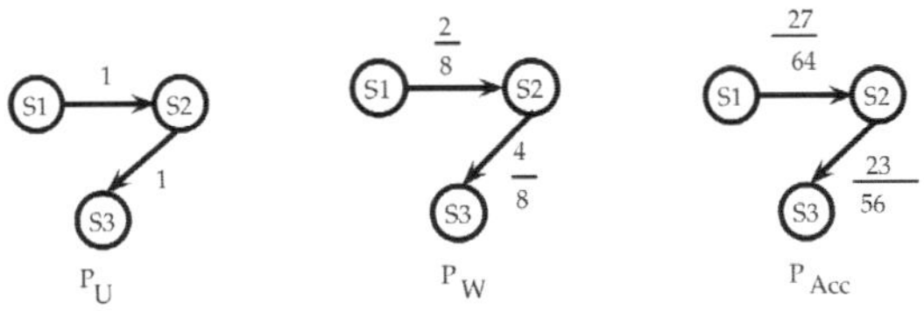

Figure 6: Normalized projections

4 Experiments

We compare the normalized entity graph with the entity graph on all tasks, Guinaudeau and Strube (2013) compared their work with the entity grid (Barzilay and Lapata, 2008; Elsner and Charniak, 2011): sentence ordering, summary coherence rating and readability assessment. Following Guinaudeau and Strube (2013) we test statistical significance with the Student's t-test and Bonferroni correction, to check whether the best result (bold value in the tables) is significantly different from the results of the entity graph and the normalized entity graph. Diacritics ** indicate significance level 0.01, * indicates significance level 0.05.

	Acc	F
Random	0.496	0.496
B&L	0.877	0.877
E&C	0.915	0.915
	Entity graph, G&S	
P_U, *Dist*	0.830	0.830**
P_W, *Dist*	0.871	0.871
P_{Acc}, *Dist*	0.889	0.889
	Normalized entity graph	
P_U, *Dist*	0.830	0.830**
P_W, *Dist*	0.886	0.886
P_{Acc}, *Dist*	**0.909**	**0.909**

Table 1: Discrimination, baselines and entity graph vs. normalized entity graph

4.1 Sentence Ordering

This task consists of two subtasks: discrimination and insertion. In both subtasks we evaluate whether our model can distinguish between the correct order of sentences in a document and an incorrect one. Experimental setup and data follow Guinaudeau and Strube (2013) (61 documents from the English test part of the CoNLL 2012 shared task (Pradhan et al., 2012)).

For discrimination we use 20 permutations of each text. Table 1 shows the results. Results for Guinaudeau and Strube (2013), G&S, are reproduced, results for Barzilay and Lapata (2008), B&L, and Elsner and Charniak (2011), E&C, were reproduced by Guinaudeau and Strube (2013).

The unweighted graph, P_U, does not need normalization. Hence the results for the entity graph and the normalized entity graph are identical. Normalization improves the results for the weighted graphs P_W and P_{Acc} with P_{Acc} outperforming B&L considerably and closely approaching E&L.

Sentence insertion is more difficult than discrimination. Following Elsner and Charniak (2011), we use two measures for evaluation: Accuracy (Acc.) and the average proportion of correct insertions per document (Ins.).

	Acc.	Ins.
Random	0.028	0.071
E&C	0.068	0.167
	Entity graph, G&S	
P_U, *Dist*	0.062**	0.101**
P_W, *Dist*	0.075	0.114**
P_{Acc}, *Dist*	0.071	0.102**
	Normalized entity graph	
P_U, *Dist*	0.062**	0.101**
P_W, *Dist*	**0.085**	**0.154**
P_{Acc}, *Dist*	0.077	0.157

Table 2: Insertion, baselines and entity graph vs. normalized entity graph

	Acc.	F
B&L	0.833	
	Entity graph, G&S	
P_U	0.800	0.815
P_W	0.613	0.613*
P_{Acc}	0.700	0.704
	Normalized entity graph	
P_U	**0.800**	**0.815**
P_W	0.775	0.775
P_{Acc}	0.788	0.788

Table 3: Summary Coherence Rating, B&L and entity graph vs. normalized entity graph

Table 2 shows that the normalized entity graph outperforms the entity graph for P_W and P_{Acc} (again, no difference for P_U). The normalized entity graph outperforms E&C in Acc. and approaches it in Ins. The high value for Ins. shows that if the normalized entity graph makes false decisions they are closer to the original ordering than the mistakes of the entity graph.

4.2 Summary Coherence Rating

We follow Barzilay and Lapata (2008) for evaluating whether the normalized entity graph can decide whether automatic or human summaries are more coherent (80 pairs of summaries extracted from DUC 2003). Human coherence scores are associated with each pair of summarized documents (Barzilay and Lapata, 2008).

Table 3 displays reported results of $B\&L$ and reproduced results of the entity graph and our normalized entity graph. Normalizing significantly improves the results for P_W and P_{Acc}. P_U is still slightly better than both, but in contrast to the entity graph, this difference is not statistically significant. We believe that better weighting schemes based on linguistic insights eventually will outperform P_U and B&L (left for future work). Distance information always degrades the results for this task (see Guinaudeau and Strube (2013)).

4.3 Readability Assessment

Readability assessment aims to distinguish texts which are difficult to read from texts which are easier to read. In experiments, Barzilay and Lapata (2008) assume that articles taken from Encyclopedia Britannica are more difficult to read (less coherent) than the corresponding articles from Encyclopedia Britannica Elementary, its version for children. We follow them with regard to data (107 article pairs), experimental setup and evaluation.

Table 4 compares reported results by Schwarm and Ostendorf (2005), S&O, Barzilay and Lapata (2008), B&L, a combined method, B&L + S&O, reproduced results for the entity graph, G&S, and our normalized entity graph. Distance information always improves the results.

	Acc.	F
S&O	0.786	
B&L	0.509	
B&L + S&O	0.888	
	Entity graph, G&S	
$P_U, Dist$	0.589	0.589**
$P_W, Dist$	0.570	0.570**
$P_{Acc}, Dist$	0.766	0.766**
	Normalized entity graph	
$P_U, Dist$	0.589	0.589**
$P_W, Dist$	**0.897**	**0.897**
$P_{Acc}, Dist$	0.850	0.850

Table 4: Readability assessment, baselines and entity graph vs. normalized entity graph

Sentences in the *Britannica Elementary* are simpler and shorter than in the *Encyclopedia Britannica*. The entity graph does not take into account the effect of entities not shared between sentences while the normalized entity graph assigns a lower weight if there are more of these entities. Hence, *Britannica Elementary* receives a higher cohesion score than *Encyclopedia Britannica* in our model. Adding grammatical information, does not help, because of the influence of the number of entities (shared and not shared) outweighs the influence of syntactic roles. The normalized entity graph ($P_W, Dist$) does not only outperform the entity graph (significantly) and B&L but also S&O and the combination B&L + S&O.

5 Conclusion

We proposed a normalization method for the entity graph (Guinaudeau and Strube, 2013). We compared our model to the entity graph and to the entity grid (Barzilay and Lapata, 2008) and showed that normalization improves the results significantly in most tasks. Future work will include adding more linguistic information, stronger weighting schemes and application to other readability datasets (Pitler and Nenkova, 2008; De Clercq et al., 2014).

Acknowledgments

This work has been funded by the Klaus Tschira Foundation, Heidelberg, Germany. The first author has been supported by a Heidelberg Institute for Theoretical Studies Ph.D. scholarship.

References

Regina Barzilay and Mirella Lapata. 2005. Modeling local coherence: An entity-based approach. In *Proceedings of the 43rd Annual Meeting of the Association for Computational Linguistics,* Ann Arbor, Mich., 25–30 June 2005, pages 141–148.

Regina Barzilay and Mirella Lapata. 2008. Modeling local coherence: An entity-based approach. *Computational Linguistics*, 34(1):1–34.

Orphée De Clercq, Véronique Hoste, Bart Desmet, Philip Van Oosten, Martine De Cock, and Lieve Macken. 2014. Using the crowd for readability prediction. *Natural Language Engineering*, 20(3):293–325.

Micha Elsner and Eugene Charniak. 2011. Extending the entity grid with entity-specific features. In *Proceedings of the 49th Annual Meeting of the Association for Computational Linguistics (Volume 2: Short Papers),* Portland, Oreg., 19–24 June 2011, pages 125–129.

Barbara J. Grosz, Aravind K. Joshi, and Scott Weinstein. 1995. Centering: A framework for modeling the local coherence of discourse. *Computational Linguistics*, 21(2):203–225.

Camille Guinaudeau and Michael Strube. 2013. Graph-based local coherence modeling. In *Proceedings of the 51st Annual Meeting of the Association for Computational Linguistics (Volume 1: Long Papers),* Sofia, Bulgaria, 4–9 August 2013, pages 93–103.

Mark E.J. Newman. 2004. Analysis of weighted networks. *Physical Review E*, 70(5):056131.

Mark E.J. Newman. 2010. *Networks: An Introduction*. Oxford University Press, New York, N.Y.

Emily Pitler and Ani Nenkova. 2008. Revisiting readability: A unified framework for predicting text quality. In *Proceedings of the 2008 Conference on Empirical Methods in Natural Language Processing,* Waikiki, Honolulu, Hawaii, 25–27 October 2008, pages 186–195.

Sameer Pradhan, Alessandro Moschitti, Nianwen Xue, Olga Uryupina, and Yuchen Zhang. 2012. CoNLL-2012 Shared Task: Modeling multilingual unrestricted coreference in OntoNotes. In *Proceedings of the Shared Task of the 16th Conference on Computational Natural Language Learning,* Jeju Island, Korea, 12–14 July 2012, pages 1–40.

Henning Rode. 2008. *From document to entity retrieval: Improving precision and performance of focused text search*. Ph.D. thesis, Enschede, June.

Sarah E. Schwarm and Mari Ostendorf. 2005. Reading level assessment using support vector machines and statistical language models. In *Proceedings of the 43rd Annual Meeting of the Association for Computational Linguistics,* Ann Arbor, Mich., 25–30 June 2005, pages 523–530.

Sally Stoddard. 1991. *Text and Texture: Patterns of Cohesion*. Ablex, Norwood, N.J.

Song Yang and David Knoke. 2001. Optimal connections: Strength and distance in valued graphs. *Social networks*, 23(4):285–295.

Tao Zhou, Jie Ren, Matúš Medo, and Yi-Cheng Zhang. 2008. Bipartite network projection and personal recommendation. *Physical Review E*, 76(4). 046115.

Katharina A. Zweig and Michael Kaufmann. 2011. A systematic approach to the one-mode projection of bipartite graphs. *Social Network Analysis and Mining*, 1:187–218.

Exploiting Timegraphs in Temporal Relation Classification

Natsuda Laokulrat†, Makoto Miwa‡, and Yoshimasa Tsuruoka†

†The University of Tokyo, 3-7-1 Hongo, Bunkyo-ku, Tokyo, Japan
{natsuda,tsuruoka}@logos.t.u-tokyo.ac.jp
‡Toyota Technological Institute, 2-12-1 Hisakata, Tempaku-ku, Nagoya, Japan
miwa@toyota-ti.ac.jp

Abstract

Most of the recent work on machine learning-based temporal relation classification has been done by considering only a given pair of temporal entities (events or temporal expressions) at a time. Entities that have temporal connections to the pair of temporal entities under inspection are not considered even though they provide valuable clues to the prediction. In this paper, we present a new approach for exploiting knowledge obtained from nearby entities by making use of timegraphs and applying the stacked learning method to the temporal relation classification task. By performing 10-fold cross validation on the Timebank corpus, we achieved an F1 score of 59.61% based on the graph-based evaluation, which is 0.16 percentage points higher than that of the local approach. Our system outperformed the state-of-the-art system that utilizes global information and achieved about 1.4 percentage points higher accuracy.

1 Introduction

Temporal relationships between entities, namely temporal expressions and events, are regarded as important information for deep understanding of documents. Being able to predict temporal relations between events and temporal expressions within a piece of text can support various NLP applications such as textual entailment (Bos et al., 2005), multi-document summarization (Bollegala et al., 2010), and question answering (Ravichandran and Hovy, 2002).

Temporal relation classification, which is one of the subtasks TempEval-3 (UzZaman et al., 2013), aims to classify temporal relationships between pairs of temporal entities into one of the 14 relation types according to the TimeML specification (Pustejovsky et al., 2005), e.g., *BEFORE, AFTER, DURING,* and *BEGINS.*

The Timebank corpus introduced by Pustejovsky et al. (2003) has enabled the machine learning-based classification of temporal relationship. By learning from the annotated relation types in the documents, it is possible to predict the temporal relation of a given pair of temporal entities (Mani et al., 2006).

However, most of the existing machine learning-based systems use local information alone, i.e., they consider only a given pair of temporal entities at a time. Entities that have temporal connections to the entities in the given pair are not considered at all even though they provide valuable clues to the prediction. Hence, the local approach often produces contradictions. For instance, the system may predict that A happens before B, that B happens before C, and that A happens after C, which are mutually contradictory.

In order to tackle the contradiction problem, global approaches have been proposed by Chambers and Jurafsky (2008) and Yoshikawa et al. (2009). Chamber and Jurafsky proposed a global model based on Integer Linear Programming that combines the output of local classifiers and maximizes the global confidence scores. While they focused only on the temporal relations between events, Yoshikawa et al. proposed a Markov Logic model to jointly predict the temporal relations between events and time expressions.

In this paper, we propose an approach that utilizes timegraphs (Miller and Schubert, 1999), which represent temporal connectivity of all temporal entities in each document, for the relation classification. Our method differs from the previous work in that their methods used transition rules to enforce consistency within each triplet of relations, but our method can also work with a set consisting of more than three relations. Moreover,

In <TIMEX3 tid="t88" type="DURATION" value="P9M" temporalFunction="true" functionInDocument="NONE" endPoint="t0">**the first nine months**</TIMEX3>**, profit** <EVENT eid="e30" class="OCCURRENCE">**rose**</EVENT> **10% to $313.2 million, or $3.89 a share, from $283.9 million, or $3.53 a share.**

<MAKEINSTANCE eventID="e30" eiid="ei349" tense="PAST" aspect="NONE" polarity="POS" pos="VERB" />

<TLINK lid="l23" relType="DURING" eventInstanceID="ei349" relatedToTime="t88" />

Figure 1: An example from the Timebank corpus

in our work, the full set of temporal relations specified in TimeML are used, rather than the reduced set used in the previous work.

We evaluate our method on the TempEval-3's Task C-relation-only data, which provides a system with all the appropriate temporal links and only needs the system to classify the relation types. The result shows that by exploiting the timegraph features in the stacked learning approach, the classification performance improves significantly. By performing 10-fold cross validation on the Timebank corpus, we can achieve an F1 score of 59.61% based on the graph-based evaluation, which is 0.16 percentage points (*pp*) higher than that of the local approach. We compared the results of our system to those of Yoshikawa et al. (2009) and achieved about 1.4 *pp* higher accuracy.

The remainder of the paper is organized as follows. Section 2 explains the temporal relation classification task and the pairwise classifier. Section 3 and Section 4 describe our proposed timegraph features and the application to the stacked learning approach. Section 5 shows the experiment setup and presents the results. Finally, we discuss the results in 6 and conclude with directions for future work in Section 7.

2 Temporal Relation Classification

According to TempEval-3, a temporal annotation task consists of several subtasks, including temporal expression extraction (Task A), event extraction (Task B), and temporal link identification and relation classification (Task C). Our work, as with the previous work mentioned in Section 1, only focuses on the relation classification task (Task C-relation only). The system does not extract events and temporal expressions automatically.

A pair of temporal entities, including events and temporal expressions, that is annotated as a temporal relation is called a TLINK. Temporal relation classification is a task to classify TLINKs into temporal relation types.

Following TempEval-3, all possible TLINKs are between:

- Event and Document Creation Time (DCT)
- Events in the same sentence
- Event and temporal expression in the same sentence
- Events in consecutive sentences

2.1 The Timebank corpus

The Timebank corpus is a human-annotated corpus commonly used in training and evaluating a temporal relation classifier. It is annotated following the TimeML specification to indicate events, temporal expressions, and temporal relations. It also provides five attributes, namely, *class, tense, aspect, modality,* and *polarity*, associated with each event *(EVENT)*, and four attributes, namely, *type, value, functionInDocument,* and *temporalFunction*, associated with each temporal expression *(TIMEX3)*. An example of the annotated event and temporal expression is shown in Figure 1. The sentence is brought from wsj_0292.tml in the Timebank corpus.

There is no modal word in the sentence, so the attribute *modality* does not appear.

We use the complete set of the TimeML relations, which has 14 types of temporal relations including *BEFORE, AFTER, IMMEDIATELY BEFORE, IMMEDIATELY AFTER, INCLUDES, IS INCLUDED, DURING, DURING INVERSE, SIMULTANEOUS, IDENTITY, BEGINS, BEGUN BY, END,* and *ENDED BY.* However, in TempEval-3, *SIMULTANEOUS* and *IDENTITY* are regarded as the same relation type, so we change all *IDENTITY* relations into *SIMULTANEOUS*.

Given the example mentioned above, the temporal relation is annotated as shown in the last line of Figure 1. From the annotated relation, the event **rose (e30)** happens *DURING* the temporal expression **the first nine months (t88)**.

Feature	E-E	E-T	Description
Event attributes			
Class	X	X	All attributes associated with events. The explanation of each attribute can be found in (Pustejovsky et al., 2005).
Tense	X	X	
Aspect	X	X	
Modality	X	X	
Polarity	X	X	
Timex attributes			
Type		X	All attributes associated with temporal expressions. The explanation of each attribute can be found in (Pustejovsky et al., 2005).
Value		X	
FunctionInDocument		X	
TemporalFunction		X	
Morphosyntactic information			
Words	X	X	Words, POS, lemmas within a window before/after event words extracted using Stanford coreNLP (Stanford NLP Group, 2012)
Part of speech tags	X	X	
Lemmas	X	X	
Lexical semantic information			
Synonyms of event word tokens	X	X	WordNet lexical database (Fellbaum, 1998)
Synonyms of temporal expressions		X	
Event-Event information			
Class match	X		Details are described in (Chambers et al., 2007)
Tense match	X		
Aspect match	X		
Class bigram	X		
Tense bigram	X		
Aspect bigram	X		
Same sentence	X	X	True if both temporal entities are in the same sentence
Deep syntactic information			
Phrase structure	X	X	Deep syntactic information extracted from Enju Parser (Miyao and Tsujii, 2008). The details are described in (Laokulrat et al., 2013)
Predicate-argument structure	X	X	

Table 1: Local features

Feature	E-E	E-T	Description
Adjacent nodes and links	X	X	The details are described in Subsection 3.2
Other paths	X	X	
Generalized paths	X	X	
(E,V,E) tuples	X	X	
(V,E,V) tuples	X	X	

Table 2: Timegraph features

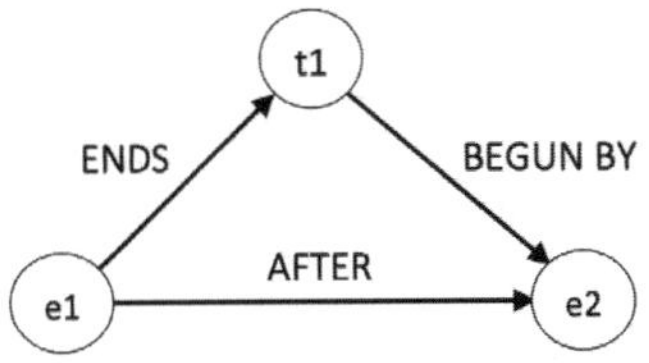

Figure 2: path length ≤ 2

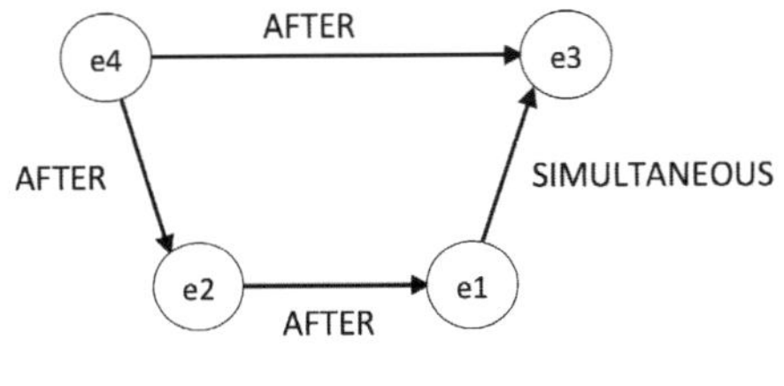

Figure 3: path length ≤ 3

3 Proposed method

Rather than using only local information on two entities in a TLINK, our goal is to exploit more global information which can be extracted from a document's timegraph. Our motivation is that temporal relations of nearby TLINKs in a timegraph provide very useful information for predicting the relation type of a given TLINK. For instance, consider the following sentence and the temporal connectivity shown in Figure 2.

About 500 people ***attended (e1)*** *a Sunday night memorial for the Buffalo-area physician who performed abortions,* ***one year (t1)*** *after he was* ***killed (e2)*** *by a sniper's bullet.*

It can be seen that the relation between ***e1*** and ***t1*** and the relation between ***t1*** and ***e2*** are useful for predicting the relation between ***e1*** and ***e2***.

Another more-complicated example is shown below with temporal connectivity in Figure 3.

"The Congress of the United States is ***affording(e1)*** *Elian Gonzalez what INS and this administration has not, which is his legal right and his right to due process,"* ***said(e2)*** *Jorge Mas Santos, chairman of the Cuban American National Foundation. "This* ***gives(e3)*** *him the protection that he will not be* ***repatriated(e4)*** *to Cuba between now and Feb. 10."*

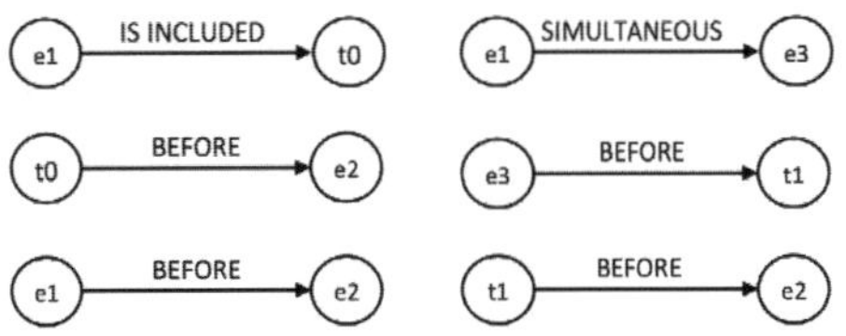

Figure 5: Local pairwise classification. Each TLINK is classified separately.

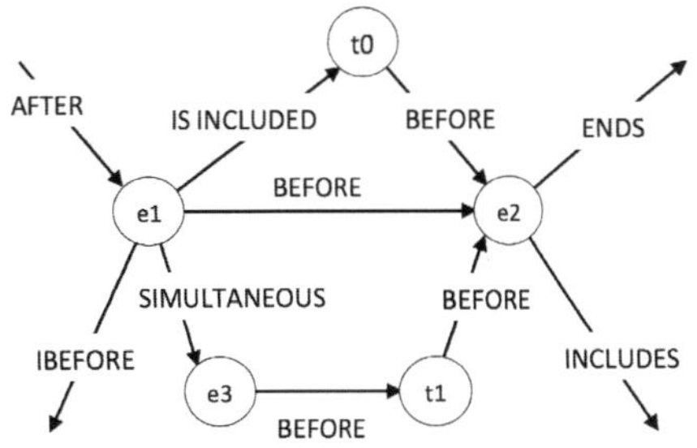

Figure 6: Timegraph constructed from a document's TLINKs

Again, the relation between ***e4*** and ***e3*** can be inferred from the nearby relations, i.e., (1) ***e4_AFTER_e2*** and ***e2_AFTER_e1*** imply ***e4_AFTER_e1***, (2) ***e4_AFTER_e1*** and ***e1_SIMULTANEOUS_e3*** imply ***e4_AFTER_e3***.

3.1 Overview of our framework

Our framework is based on the stacked learning method (Wolpert, 1992), which employs two stages of classification as illustrated in Figure 4.

3.1.1 Local pairwise model

In a local pairwise model, temporal relation classification is done by considering only a given pair of temporal entities at a time as illustrated in Figure 5. We use a supervised machine learning approach and employ the basic feature set that can be easily extracted from the document's text and the set of features proposed in our previous work (Laokulrat et al., 2013), which utilizes deep syntactic information, as baselines. The local features at different linguistic levels are listed in Table 1.

Two classifiers are used: one for Event-Event TLINKs (E-E), and the other for Event-Time TLINKs (E-T).

3.1.2 Stacked learning

Stacked learning is a machine learning method that enables the learner to be aware of the labels of nearby examples.

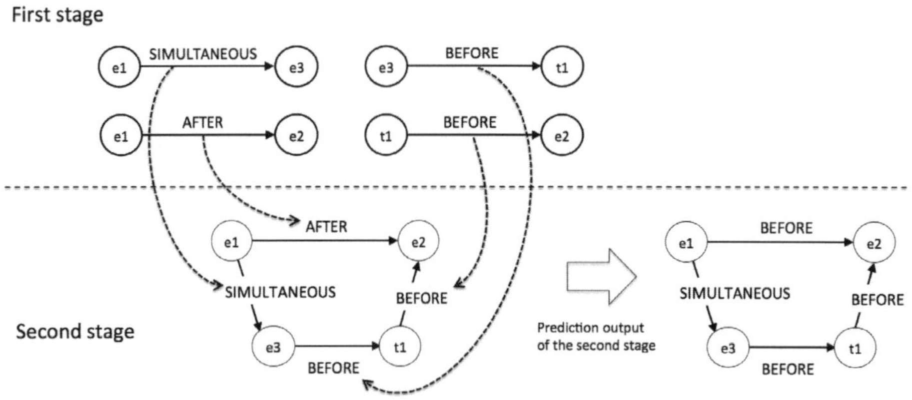

Figure 4: Stacked learning. The output from the first stage is treated as features for the second stage. The final output is predicted using label information of nearby TLINKs.

The first stage, as shown in Figure 5, uses the local classifiers and predicts the relation types of all TLINKs. In the second stage, the document's timegraph is constructed and the output from the first stage is associated with TLINKs in the graph. The classifiers in the second stage use the information from the nearby TLINKs and predict the final output. We exploit features extracted from the documents' timegraphs, as listed in Section 3.2 in the second stage of the stacked learning.

An example of a document's timegraph is shown in Figure 6.

3.2 Timegraph features

We treat timegraphs as directed graphs and double the number of edges by adding new edges with opposite relation types/directions to every existing edge. For example, if the graph contains an edge ***e1**_BEFORE_**e2***, we add a new edge ***e2**_AFTER_**e1***.

Our proposed timegraph features are described below.

- Adjacent nodes and links

  The features are the concatenation of the directions to the adjacent links to the pair of entities, the relation types of the links, and the information on the adjacent nodes, i.e., word tokens, part of speech tags, lemmas. For example, the features for predicting the relation between ***e1*** and ***e2*** in Figure 6 are *SRC_OUT-IS_INCLUDED-*(Type of ***t0***), *DEST_IN-BEFORE-*(Type of ***t0***), and so on.

  In this work, only Type of temporal expression (an attribute given in the Timebank corpus), Tense and Part-of-speech tag are applied but other attributes could also be used.

- Other paths

  Paths with certain path lengths (in this work, $2 \leq$ path length ≤ 4) between the temporal entities are used as features. The paths must not contain cycles. For example, the path features of the relation between ***e1*** and ***e2*** are *IS_INCLUDED-BEFORE* and *SIMULTANEOUS-BEFORE-BEFORE*.

- Generalized paths

  A generalized version of the path features, e.g., the *IS_INCLUDED-BEFORE* path is generalized to **-BEFORE* and *IS_INCLUDED-**.

- (E,V,E) tuples

  The (E,V,E) tuples of the edges and vertices on the path are used as features, e.g., *IS_INCLUDED_*(Type of ***t0***)*_BEFORE*.

- (V,E,V) tuples

  The (V,E,V) tuples of the edges and vertices on the path are used as features, e.g., (Tense of ***e1***)*_IS INCLUDED_*(Type of ***t0***) and (Type of ***t0***)*_BEFORE_*(Tense of ***e2***).

The summary of the timegraph features is shown in Table 2.

4 Relation inference and time-time connection

We call TLINKs that have more than one path between the temporal entities *"multi-path TLINKs"*. The coverage of the multi-path TLINKs is presented in Table 3. The annotated entities in the Timebank corpus create loosely connected timegraphs as we can see from the table that only 5.65% of all the annotated TLINKs have multiple paths between given pairs of temporal entities.

Since most of the timegraph features are only applicable for multi-path TLINKs, it is important to have dense timegraphs. In order to increase the numbers of connections, we employ two approaches: relation inference and time-time connection.

4.1 Relation inference

We create new E-E and E-T connections between entities in a timegraph by following a set of inference rules. For example, if ***e1*** happens *AFTER* ***e2*** and ***e2*** happens *IMMEDIATELY_AFTER* ***e3***, then we infer a new temporal relation "***e1*** happens *AFTER* ***e3***". In this paper, we add a new connection only when the inference gives only one type of temporal relation as a result from the relation inference. Figure 7b shows the timegraph after adding new inference relations to the original timegraph in Figure 7a.

4.2 Time-time connection

As with Chambers et al. (2007) and Tatu and Srikanth (2008), we also create new connections between time entities in a timegraph by applying some rules to normalized values of time entities provided in the corpus.

Figure 7c shows the timegraph after adding a time-time link and new inference relations to the original timegraph in Figure 7a. When the normalized value of ***t2*** is more than the value of ***t1***, a TLINK with the relation type *AFTER* is added between them. After that, as introduced in Subsection 4.2, new inference relations (***e1-e2***, ***e1-e3***, ***e2-e3***) are added.

As the number of relations grows too large after performing time-time connection and inference relation recursively, we limited the number of TLINKs for each document's timegraph to 10,000 relations. The total number of TLINKs for all documents in the corpus is presented in Table 4. The first row is the number of the human-annotated relations. The second and third rows show the total number after performing relation inference and time-time connection.

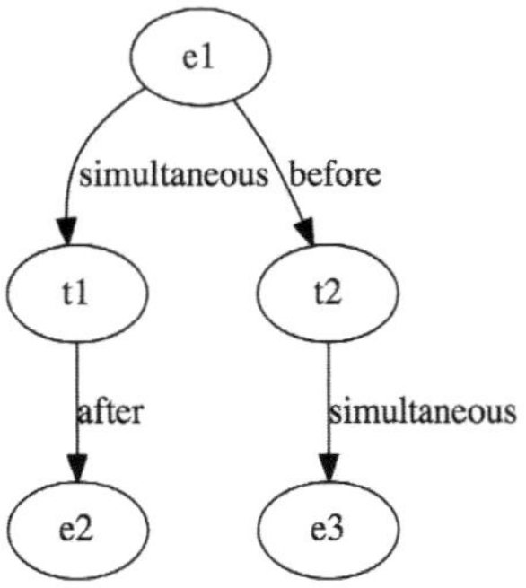

(a) Original timegraph

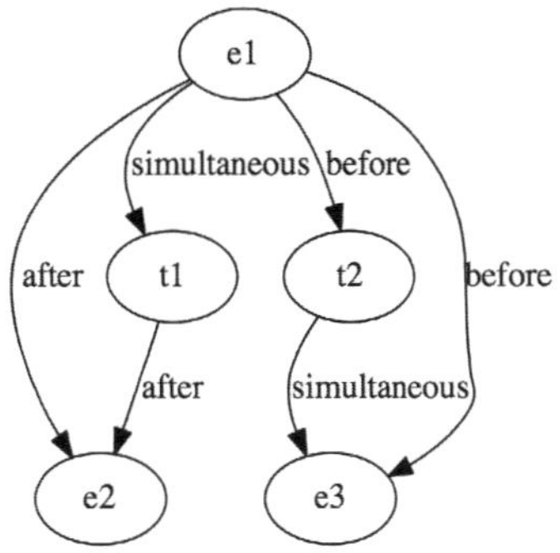

(b) After relation inference. Two relations (e1-e2, e1-e3) are added.

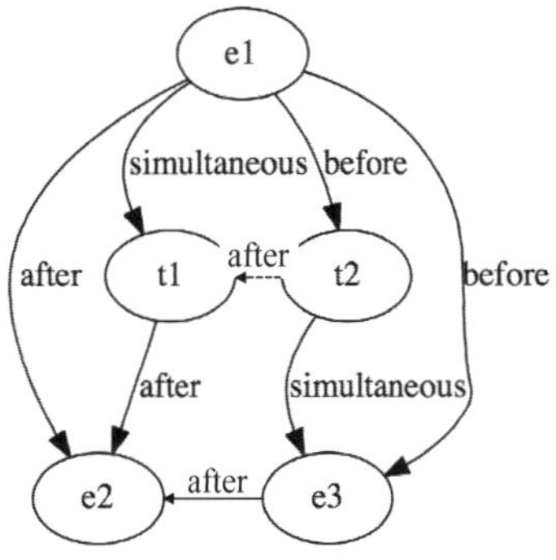

(c) After time-time connection (t1-t2) and relation inference. Three relations (e1-e2, e1-e3, e2-e3) are added.

Figure 7: Increasing number of TLINKs

No. of TLINKs	**E-E**	**E-T**	**Total**
All TLINKs	2,520	2,463	4,983
Multi-path TLINKs	119	163	282
Percentage	4.72	6.62	5.65

Table 3: Coverage of multi-path TLINKs

Approach	Graph-based evaluation		
	F1(%)	P(%)	R(%)
Local - baseline features	58.15	58.17	58.13
Local - baseline + deep features	59.45	59.48	59.42
Stacked - baseline features	58.33	58.37	58.29
Stacked (inference) - baseline features	58.30	58.32	58.27
Stacked (inference, time-time) - baseline features	58.29	58.31	58.27
Stacked - baseline + deep features	59.55	59.51	59.58
Stacked (inference) - baseline + deep features	59.55	59.57	59.52
Stacked (inference, time-time) - baseline + deep features	**59.61**	**59.63**	**59.58**

Table 5: Ten-fold cross validation results on the training set

No. of TLINKs	Total
Annotated	4,983
+Inference	24,788
+Inference + time-time connection	87,992

Table 4: Number of TLINKs in the Timebank corpus

5 Evaluation

For the baselines and both stages of the stacked learning, we have used the LIBLINEAR (Fan et al., 2008) and configured it to work as L2-regularized logistic regression classifiers.

We trained our models on the Timebank corpus, introduced in Subsection 2.1, which was provided by the TempEval-3 organiser. The corpus contains 183 newswire articles in total.

5.1 Results on the training data

The performance analysis is performed based on 10-fold cross validation over the training data. The classification F1 score improves by 0.18 *pp* and 0.16 *pp* compared to the local pairwise models with/without deep syntactic features.

We evaluated the system using a graph-based evaluation metric proposed by UzZaman and Allen (2011). Table 5 shows the classification accuracy over the training set using graph-based evaluation.

The stacked model affected the relation classification output of the local model, changing the relation types of 390 (out of 2520) E-E TLINKs and 169 (out of 2463) E-T TLINKs.

5.2 Comparison with the state of the art

We compared our system to that of Yoshikawa et al. (2009) which uses global information to improve the accuracy of temporal relation classification. Their system was evaluated based on TempEval-2's rules and data set (Verhagen et al., 2007), in which the relation types were reduced to six relations: *BEFORE*, *OVERLAP*, *AFTER*, *BEFORE-OR-OVERLAP*, *OVERLAP-OR-AFTER*, and *VAGUE*. The evaluation was done using 10-fold cross validation over the same data set as that of their reported results.

According to TempEval-2's rules, there are three tasks as follows:

- Task A: Temporal relations between events and all time expressions appearing in the same sentence.
- Task B: Temporal relations between events and the DCT.
- Task C: Temporal relations betweeen main verbs of adjacent sentences.

The number of TLINKs annotated by the organizer, after relation inference, and after time-time connection for each task is summarized in Table 7. Table 8 shows the number of TLINKs after performing relation inference and time-time connection.

As shown in Table 6, our system can achieve better results in task B and C even without deep syntactic features but performs worse than their system in task A. Compared to the baselines, the overall improvement is statistically significant* ($p < 10^{-4}$, McNemar's test, two-tailed) without deep syntactic features and gets more statistically significant** ($p < 10^{-5}$, McNemar's test, two-tailed) when applying deep syntactic information to the system. The overall result has about 1.4 *pp* higher accuracy than the result from their global model. Note that Yoshikawa et al. (2009) did not apply deep syntactic features in their system.

Approach	Task A	Task B	Task C	Overall
Yoshikawa et al. (2009) (local)	61.3	78.9	53.3	66.7
Yoshikawa et al. (2009) (global)	66.2	79.9	55.2	68.9
Our system (local) - baseline features	59.9	80.3	58.5	68.5
Our system (local) - baseline + deep features	62.1	80.3	58.4	69.0
Our system (stacked) - baseline features	59.5	79.9	58.5	68.2
Our system (stacked, inference) - baseline features	59.9	80.0	**59.7**	68.7
Our system (stacked, inference, time-time) - baseline features	63.8	80.0	58.9	69.5*
Our system (stacked) - baseline + deep features	63.5	79.4	58.0	68.9
Our system (stacked, inference) - baseline + deep features	63.7	80.3	59.2	69.7
Our system (stacked, inference, time-time) - baseline + deep features	**65.9**	**80.5**	58.9	**70.3****

Table 6: Comparison of the stacked model to the state of the art and to our local model (F1 score(%))

No. of TLINKs	Task A	Task B	Task C
Annotated	1,490	2,556	1,744

Table 7: TempEval-2 data set

No. of TLINKs	Total
Annotated	5,970
+Inference	156,654
+Inference + time-time connection	167,875

Table 8: Number of relations in TempEval-2 data set

The stacked model enhances the classification accuracy of task A when timegraphs are dense enough. Deep syntactic features can be extracted only when temporal entities are in the same sentences so they improve the model for task A (event-time pairs in the same sentences) but these features clearly lower the accuracy of task C, since there are very few event-event pairs that appear in the same sentences (and break the definition of task C). This is probably because the sparseness of the deep features degrades the performance in task C. Moreover, these features do not help task B in the local model because we cannot extract any deep syntactic features from TLINKs between events and DCT. However, they contribute slightly to the improvement in the stacked model since deep syntactic features increase the accuracy of the prediction of task A in the first stage of the stacked model. As a result, timegraph features extracted from the output of the first stage are better than those extracted from the local model trained on only baseline features.

6 Discussion

As we can see from Table 5 and 6, although deep syntactic features can improve the classification accuracy significantly, some additional preprocessing is required. Moreover, deep parsers are not able to parse sentences in some specific domains. Thus, sometimes it is not practical to use this kind of features in real-world temporal relation classification problems. By applying the stacked learning approach to the temporal relation classification task, the system with only baseline features is able to achieve good classification results compared to the system with deep syntactic features.

Again, from Table 5 and 6, the inference and time-time connection, described in Section 4, sometimes degrade the performance. This is presumably because the number of features increases severely as the number of TLINKs increased.

The stacked model also has another advantage that it is easy to build and does not consume too much training time compared to MLNs used by Yoshikawa et al. (2009), which are, in general, computationally expensive and infeasible for large training sets.

7 Conclusion

In this paper, we present an approach for exploiting timegraph features in the temporal relation classification task. We employ the stacked learning approach to make use of information obtained from nearby entities in timegraphs. The results show that our system can outperform the state-of-the-art system and achieve good accuracy by using only baseline features. We also apply the relation inference rules and the time-time connection to tackle the timegraphs' sparseness problem.

In future work, we hope to improve the classification performance by making use of probability values of prediction results obtained from the first stage of the stacked learning and applying the full set of inference relations to the system.

Acknowledgement

The authors would like to thank the anonymous reviewers for their insightful comments and suggestions, which were helpful in improving the quality of the paper.

References

Danushka Bollegala, Naoaki Okazaki, and Mitsuru Ishizuka. 2010. A bottom-up approach to sentence ordering for multi-document summarization. In *Information Processing & Management*, Volume 46, Issue 1, January 2010, pages 89–109.

Johan Bos and Katja Markert. 2005. Recognising textual entailment with logical inference. In *HLT/EMNLP 2005*, pages 628–635.

Nathanael Chambers, Shan Wang and Dan Jurafsky. 2007. Classifying temporal relations between events. In *ACL 2007*, pages 173–176.

Nathanael Chambers and Dan Jurafsky. 2008. Jointly combining implicit constraints improves temporal ordering. In *EMNLP 2008*, pages 698–706.

Rong-En Fan, Kai-Wei Chang, Cho-Jui Hsieh, Xiang-Rui Wang, and Chih-Jen Lin. 2008. LIBLINEAR: A library for large linear classification.

Christiane Fellbaum. 1998. WordNet: An Electronic Lexical Database. Cambridge, MA: MIT Press.

Natsuda Laokulrat, Makoto Miwa, Yoshimasa Tsuruoka and Takashi Chikayama. 2013. UTTime: Temporal relation classification using deep syntactic features. In *SemEval 2013*, pages 89–92.

Inderjeet Mani, Marc Verhagen, Ben Wellner, Chong Min Lee and James Pustejovsky. 2006. Machine Learning of Temporal Relations. In *ACL 2006*, pages 753–760.

Stephanie A. Miller and Lenhart K. Schubert. 1999. Time revisited. In *Computational Intelligence 6*, pages 108–118.

Yusuke Miyao and Jun'ichi Tsujii. 2008. Feature forest models for probabilistic HPSG parsing. In *Computational Linguistics*. 34(1). pages 35–80, MIT Press.

James Pustejovsky, Patrick Hanks, Roser Saurí, Andew See, Rob Gaizauskas, Andrea Setzer, Dragomir Radev, Beth Sundheim, David Day, Lisa Ferro and Marcia Lazo. 2003. The TIMEBANK Corpus. In *Proceedings of Corpus Linguistics 2003 (March 2003)*, pages 545–557.

James Pustejovsky, Robert Ingria, Roser Saurí, José Castaño, Jessica Littman, Rob Gaizauskas, Andrea Setzer, Graham Katz and Inderjeet Mani. 2005. The specification language TimeML. In *The Language of Time: A reader*, pages 545–557.

Deepak Ravichandran and Eduard Hovy. 2002. Learning surface text patterns for a question answering system. In *ACL 2002*, pages 41–47.

Stanford Natural Language Processing Group. 2012. Stanford CoreNLP.

Marta Tatu and Munirathnam Srikanth. 2008. Experiments with reasoning for temporal relations between events. In *COLING 2008*, pages 857–864.

Naushad UzZaman and James F. Allen. 2011. Temporal evaluation. In *ACL 2011*, pages 351–356.

Naushad UzZaman, Hector Llorens, Leon Derczynski, Marc Verhagen, James Allen and James Pustejovsky. 2013. SemEval-2013 Task 1: TempEval-3: Evaluating time expressions, events, and temporal relations. In *SemEval 2013*, pages 2–9.

Marc Verhagen, Robert Gaizauskas, Frank Schilder, Mark Hepple, Graham Katz and James Pustejovsky. 2007. SemEval-2007 task 15: TempEval temporal relation identification. In *SemEval 2007*, pages 75–80.

David H. Wolpert. 1992. Stacked generalization. In *Neural Networks*, volume 5, pages 241–259.

Katsumasa Yoshikawa, Sebastian Riedel ,Masayuki Asahara and Yuji Matsumoto. 2009. Jointly identifying temporal relations with Markov Logic. In *ACL 2009*, pages 405–413.

Multi-document Summarization Using Bipartite Graphs

Daraksha Parveen and **Michael Strube**
Heidelberg Institute for Theoretical Studies gGmbH
Schloss-Wolfsbrunnenweg 35
69118 Heidelberg, Germany
(daraksha.parveen|michael.strube)@h-its.org

Abstract

In this paper, we introduce a novel graph based technique for topic based multi-document summarization. We transform documents into a bipartite graph where one set of nodes represents entities and the other set of nodes represents sentences. To obtain the summary we apply a ranking technique to the bipartite graph which is followed by an optimization step. We test the performance of our method on several DUC datasets and compare it to the state-of-the-art.

1 Introduction

Topic-based multi-document summarization aims to create a single summary from a set of given documents while considering the topic of interest. The input documents can be created by querying an information retrieval or search engine for a particular topic and retaining highly ranked documents, or by clustering documents of a large collection and then using each cluster as a set of input documents (Galanis et al., 2012). Here, each cluster of the set of documents contains a representative topic.

A summary extracted from a set of input documents must be related to the topic of that set. If textual units (or sentences) extracted from different documents convey the same information, then those units are called redundant. Ideally, the multi-document summary should be non-redundant. Hence each textual unit in a summary should convey unique information. Still, all extracted textual units should be related to the topic. They should also make up a coherent summary.

When building summaries from multiple documents belonging to different sets, a system should attempt to optimize these three basic properties:

1. **Relevance**: A summary should contain only those textual units which are relevant to the topic and provide useful information.
2. **Non-redundancy**: A summary should not contain the same information twice.
3. **Readability**: A summary should have good readability (syntactically well formed, no dangling pronouns, coherent, ...).

Generally, multi-document summarization systems differ from each other on the basis of document representation, sentence selection method or on the requirements for the output summary. Popular methods for document representation include graph-based representations (e.g. *LexRank* (Erkan and Radev, 2004) and *TextRank* (Mihalcea and Tarau, 2004)) and tf-idf vector-based representations (Luhn, 1958; Nenkova and Vanderwende, 2005; Goldstein et al., 2000). These document representations act as input for the next phase and provide information about the importance of individual sentences. Sentence selection is the crucial phase of the summarizer where sentence redundancy must be handled in an efficient way. A widely used technique is the greedy approach introduced by Carbonell and Goldstein (1998) and Goldstein et al. (2000). They compute a relevance score for all sentences with regard to the topic, start by extracting the most relevant sentence, and then iteratively extract further sentences which are relevant to the topic and at the same time most dissimilar to already extracted sentences. Later more fundamental optimization methods have been widely used in multi-document summarization, e.g. Integer Linear Programming (ILP) (McDonald, 2007; Gillick et al., 2009; Nishikawa et al., 2010; Galanis et al., 2012). Unlike most other approaches (Galanis et al., 2012) has also taken into account the readability of the final summary.

In this work, we introduce an extractive topic based multi-document summarization system which represents documents graphically and optimizes the importance of sentences and non-redundancy. The importance of sentences is obtained by means of applying the Hubs and Authorities ranking algorithm (Kleinberg, 1999) on the unweighted bipartite graph whereas redundancy in the final summary is dealt with entities in a graph.

In Section 2 we introduce the state-of-the-art in topic based multi-document summarizaton. Section 3 provides a detailed description of our approach. Experiments are described in Section 4 where we also briefly describe the datasets used and the results. Section 5 discusses the results of our approach, and in Section 6 we finally give conclusions.

2 Related work

A graph-based representation of documents for summarization is adopted by various approaches. For instance, *TextRank* by Mihalcea and Tarau (2004) applies the *PageRank* algorithm (Brin and Page, 1998) to extract important sentences for single document summarization. This ranking algorithm proclaims the importance of a sentence by considering the global information which is computed recursively from the entire graph. Later, the graph is converted into a weighted graph in which the weights are calculated by measuring the similarity of sentences (Mihalcea, 2004). Similarly, in the *LexRank* approach (Erkan and Radev, 2004), documents are represented as a similarity graph in which the sentences are nodes and these sentences are then ranked according to centrality measures. The three centrality measures used are degree, *LexRank* with threshold and continuous *LexRank*. *LexRank* is a measure to calculate ranks using the similarity graph of sentences. It is also known as lexical *PageRank*. The summarization approach developed by Gong and Liu (2001) is also based on ranking sentences where important sentences are selected using a relevance measure and latent semantic analysis.

Later, for better performance, sentences are classified according to their existence in their final summary in binary format i.e. 1 (belongs to summary) and 0 (doesn't belong to summary) (Shen et al., 2007; Gong and Liu, 2001). Here, the sentences are projected as feature vectors and conditional random fields are used to classify them. During document processing, most informative sentences are selected by the summarizer (Shen et al., 2007). Fattah and Ren (2009) also considers summarization as two class classification problem. They use a genetic algorithm and mathematical regression to select appropriate weights for the features and used different classification technique for e.g. feed forward neural network, probablistic neural network and Gaussian mixture models.

In the summarization task, optimization of the three properties discussed in Section 1, relevance, non-redundancy and readability, is required. This is a global inference problem, which can be solved by two approaches. Firstly, relevance and redundancy can be optimized simultaneously. For instance, Goldstein et al. (2000) developed a metric named MMR-MD (influenced by the Maximum Marginal Relevance (MMR) approach of Carbonell and Goldstein (1998)) and applied it to clusters of passages. Similarly, influenced by the SumBasic system (Nenkova and Vanderwende, 2005), Yih et al. (2007) developed a system which assigns a score to each term on the basis of position and frequency information and selects the sentence having highest score. Other approaches are based on an estimate of word importance (e.g. Lin and Hovy (2000)) or the log likelihood ratio test which identifies the importance of words using a supervised model that considers a rich set of features (Hong and Nenkova, 2014). Finally, Barzilay and Elhadad (1999) extract sentences which are strongly connected by lexical chains for summarization. The second approach deals with relevance and redundancy seperately. For instance, McKeown et al. (1999) create clusters of similar sentences and pick the representative one from every cluster. The representative sentence of a cluster of sentences takes care of the requirement to extract relevant information whereas clustering reduces the redundancy.

McDonald (2007) proposes a new ILP optimization method for extractive summarization. He introduces an objective function which maximizes the importance of sentences and minimizes the similarity of sentences. ILP methods for optimization have also been adopted by Berg-Kirkpatrick et al. (2011),Woodsend and Lapata (2012) and Galanis et al. (2012). Until now, Galanis et al. (2012) have reported the highest scores for multi-document summarization on DUC2005 and DUC2007. However, their approach is not completely unsupervised.

3 Our method

This section describes the technique, which we adopted for summarization. We start by discussing the graphical representation of the text followed by a description how to quantify the importance of sentences in the input texts. We then discuss the ILP technique which optimizes the importance of sentences and redundancy.

3.1 Graphical representation of text

The graphical representation of a text makes it more expressive than a traditional *tf-idf* depiction for summarization. A graph can easily capture the essence of the whole text without leading to high computational complexity. Guinaudeau and Strube (2013) introduced a bipartite graph representation of text based on the entity grid (Barzilay and Lapata, 2008) representation of text. The projection of this bipartite graph representation has been used for calculating the local coherence of a text (Guinaudeau and Strube, 2013). The basic intuition to use a bipartite graph for summarization is that it contains entity transitions similar to lexical chains (Barzilay and Elhadad, 1999). An appropriate measure to determine the importance of sentences by considering strong entity transitions indicates the information central to a text better than simply giving scores on the basis of most frequent words. The unweighted bipartite graph $G = (V_s, V_e, L)$ contains two sets of nodes, V_s corresponding to the sentences from the input text and V_e corresonding to the entities, and a set of edges represented by L. Figure 1 shows a model summary from the DUC 2006 data, which is transformed into an entity grid in Figure 2 (Barzilay and Lapata, 2008; Elsner and Charniak, 2011). Here, cells are filled with the syntactic role a mention of an entity occupies in a sentence. Subjects are denoted by *S*, objects by *O* and all other roles by *X*. If an entity is not mentioned in a sentence then the corresponding cell contains "-". In the corresponding bipartite graph (Figure 3), edges are created between a sentence and an entity only if the entity is mentioned in a sentence (the cell in entity grid is not "-"). Since this is a dyadic graph, there are no edges between nodes of the same set.

3.2 Ranking the importance of sentences

A graph based ranking algorithm is used to calculate the importance of a sentence represented as a node in the graph discussed above. In contrast to the local information specific to a vertex, graphical ranking algorithms take (graph-) global information to calculate the rank of a node. The *Hyperlink-Induced Topic Search* algorithm (*HITS*, also known as *Hubs and Authorities*) by Kleinberg (1999) is used to rank sentences in our method. This algorithm considers two types of nodes, hence it is well suited to rank sentences in our bipartite graph. Entities are considered as hub nodes, and sentences are considered as authority nodes. The importance of a sentence is calculated in two steps:

- Hub update rule: Update each node's hub score to be equal to the sum of the authority scores of each node that it points to. It can be written as:

$$HubScore = A \cdot AuthorityScore \quad (1)$$

Here, A is an adjacency matrix which represents the connection between the nodes in a graph.

- Authority update rule: In this step, each authority node is updated by equating them to the sum of the hub scores of each node, which is pointing to that authority node. It can be written as:

$$AuthorityScore = A^T \cdot HubScore \quad (2)$$

Hence, the authority weight is high if it is pointed at by a hub having high weights.

Given some intial ranks to all nodes in a graph, the hub and authority update rules are applied until convergence. After applying this algorithm, the rank of every node is obtained. The rank is considered as importance of the node within the graph. We normalize the ranks of sentences according to sentence length to avoid assigning high ranks to long sentences.

To incorporate important information from documents, ranks of entities are incremented by $Rank + tf_{doc} \cdot idf_{doc}$ in every iteration, where tf_{doc} shows the importance of an entity in a document by calculating the frequency whereas idf_{doc} is an inverse document frequency from the current cluster. $Rank + tf_{doc} \cdot idf_{doc}$ is used in calculating the AuthorityScore. Initially, the $Rank$ can be any numerical value but after every iteration of the HITS algorithm it will be updated accordingly.

S_1 The treatment of osteoarthritis includes a number of non-steroidal anti-inflammatory drugs such as aspirin, acetaminophen, and ibuprofen.

S_2 These drugs, however, cause liver damage and gastrointestinal bleeding and contribute to thousands of hospitalizations and deaths per year.

S_3 New cox-2 inhibitor drugs are proven as effective against pain, with fewer gastrointestinal side effects.

S_4 The two together appeared to reduce knee pain after 8 weeks.

Figure 1: Model summary from DUC 2006

	TREATMENT (e1)	OSTEOARTHRITIS (e2)	NUMBER (e3)	DRUGS (e4)	ASPIRIN (e5)	ACETAMINOPHEN(e6)	IBUPROFEN (e7)	DAMAGE (e8)	BLEEDING (e9)	THOUSANDS (e10)	DEATHS (e11)	YEAR (e12)	PAIN (e13)	EFFECTS (e14)	TWO (e15)	WEEKS (e16)
S_1	S	X	O	X	X	X	X	-	-	-	-	-	-	-	-	-
S_2	-	-	-	S	-	-	-	O	O	X	X	X	-	-	-	-
S_3	-	-	-	S	-	-	-	-	-	-	-	-	X	X	-	-
S_4	-	-	-	-	-	-	-	-	-	-	-	-	O	-	S	X

Figure 2: Entity grid of the model summary from Figure 1

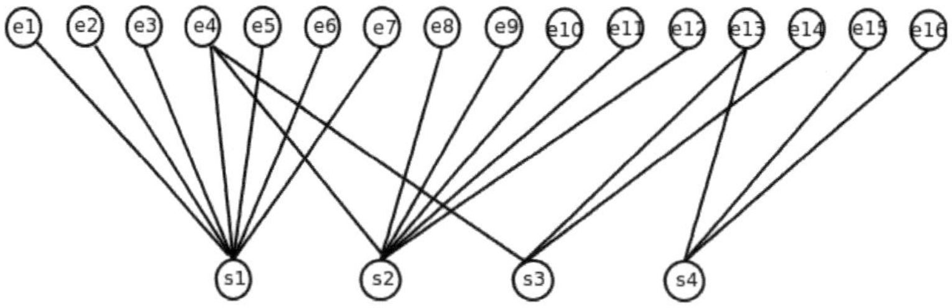

Figure 3: Bipartite graph derived from the entity grid from Figure 2

3.3 Optimization algorithm

In topic-based multi-document summarization, the final summary should be non-redundant. At the same time it should contain the important information from the documents. To achieve these two conditions, we employ integer linear programming (ILP) to obtain an optimal solution. In ILP we maximize an objective function. Our objective function, given in Equation 3, has two parts: the importance of a summary and the non-redundancy of a summary. The values obtained after ranking by the HITS algorithm are used as the importance of sentences for ILP. Non-redundancy can not be calculated for a single sentence. Instead, it has to be evaluated with respect to other sentences. We calculate non-redundancy by the number of unshared entities, i.e. entities which are not shared by other sentences, after appending a sentence to a summary. The least redundant sentence will increase the number of entities in the final summary.

$$max(\lambda_1 \sum_{i=1}^{n} (Rank(s_i) + topicsim(s_i)) \cdot x_i + \lambda_2 \sum_{j=1}^{m} y_j) \tag{3}$$

Equation 3 is the objective function where m is

	Topic	Documents per topic	Human Summaries	Word limit in final summary
DUC 2005	50	25-50	4-9	250
DUC 2006	50	25	4	250
DUC 2007	45	25	4	250

Table 1: Document Statistics

the number of entities in a document and n is the number of sentences in a document. x_i and y_j are binary variables for sentences and entities respectively. λ_1 and λ_2 are tuning parameters. $Rank(s_i)$ is a rank of a sentence s_i obtained by applying the HITS algorithm. Since, we work on topic-based multi-document summarization, we include topic information by calculating $topicsim(s_i)$, which captures the cosine similarity of a sentence s_i with the corresponding topic. If the topic contains more than one sentence then we take an average of cosine similarity with a sentence s_i. The constraints on the variables are shown in Equations 4-6:

$$\sum_{i=1}^{n} Len(s_i) \cdot x_i \leq Len(summary) \quad (4)$$

Here, $Len(s_i)$ and $Len(summary)$ are the number of words in a sentence s_i and in the final summary, respectively. This constraint does not allow the length of final summary to exceed its maximum length. The maximum length varies depending on the datasets discussed in Section 4.1.

$$\sum_{j \epsilon E_i} y_j \geq Entities(s_i), \text{for } i = 1, \ldots, n \quad (5)$$

In constraint 5, E_i is a set of entities present in a sentence s_i. The number of entities present in a sentence is represented as $Entities(s_i)$. If a sentence s_i is selected then the entities present in a sentence are also selected($\sum y_j = Entities(s_i)$). Whereas, if a sentence s_i is not selected then some of its entities can also be selected because they may appear in already selected sentences ($Entities(s_i) = 0, \therefore \sum y_j \geq 0$). In both the cases, constraint 5 is not violated.

$$\sum_{i \epsilon S_j} x_i \geq y_j, forj = 1, \ldots, m \quad (6)$$

In constraint 6, S_j is a set of sentences containing entity y_j. This constraint shows that, if an entity y_j is selected then at least one sentence is selected which contains it ($y_j = 1, \therefore \sum x_i \geq 1$). If an entity y_j is not selected, then it is possible that none of the sentences which contain it may not be selected ($y_j = 0, \therefore \sum x_i = 0$). Also, constraint 4 holds in either of the cases.

4 Experiments

We perform experiments on various DUC datasets to compare the results with state-of-the-art systems.

4.1 Datasets

Datasets used for our experiments are DUC2005 (Dang, 2005), DUC2006 (Dang, 2006) and DUC2007[1] . Each dataset contains group of related documents. Each group of documents contains one related topic or a query consisting of a few sentences. In DUC, the final summary should respond to the corresponding topic. Also, the summary cannot exceed the maximum allowed length. For instance, in DUC2005, 250 words are allowed in the final summary. Every document cluster has corresponding human summaries for evaluating system summaries on the basis of ROUGE scores (Lin, 2004). The sources of DUC datasets are Los Angeles Times, Financial Times of London, Associated Press, New York Times and Xinhua news agency. We employ ROUGE SU4 and ROUGE 2 as evaluation metrics. ROUGE returns recall, precision and F-score of a system, but usually only recall is used in for evaluating automatic summarization systems, because the final summary does not contain many words. Hence, if the recall is high then the summarization system is working well. Document statistics is provided in Table 1.

4.2 Experimental setup

We use raw documents from the various DUC datasets as input for our system. We remove non-alphabetical characters from the documents. Then we obtain a clean sentence split by means of the Stanford parser (Klein and Manning, 2003) so that the sentences are compatible with the next steps.

[1] http://www-nlpir.nist.gov/projects/duc/index.html

	ROUGE-2	ROUGE-SU4
$\lambda_1 = 0.5$ & $\lambda_2 = 0.5$	0.07950	0.14060
$\lambda_1 = 0.6$ & $\lambda_2 = 0.4$	0.07956	0.14071
$\lambda_1 = 0.7$ & $\lambda_2 = 0.3$	0.07975	0.14105
$\lambda_1 = 0.8$ & $\lambda_2 = 0.2$	0.07976	0.14106
$\lambda_1 = 0.9$ & $\lambda_2 = 0.1$	0.07985	0.14107

Table 2: Results on different λ's on DUC 2005

Dataset	ROUGE-2	ROUGE-SU4
DUC 2005 (32)	0.07975 (1)	0.14105 (1)
DUC 2006 (35)	0.08969 (3)	0.15070 (2)
DUC 2007 (32)	0.10928 (6)	0.16735 (5)

Table 3: System performance (and rank) on the DUC 2005, 2006 and 2007 (main) data. The number in parenthesis after the DUC year indicates the number of competing systems.

We use the Brown coherence toolkit (Elsner and Charniak, 2011) to convert the documents into the entity grid representation from which the bipartite graph is constructed (Guinaudeau and Strube, 2013). Entities in the graph correspond to head nouns of noun phrase mentioned in the sentences. The ranking algorithm from Section 3.2 is applied to this graph and returns the importance score of a sentence as required by the objective function given in Equation 3. Next optimization using ILP is performed as described in Section 3.3. We use GUROBI Optimizer[2]for performing ILP. ILP returns a binary value, i.e., if a sentence should be included in the summary it returns 1, if not it returns 0. We set $\lambda_1 = 0.7$ and $\lambda_2 = 0.3$ for all datasets. We did not choose the optimal values, but rather opted for ones which favor importance over non-redundancy. We did not observe significant differences between different λ values as long as $\lambda_1 > \lambda_2$ (see Table 2). The sentences in the output summary are ordered according to their ranks. If the output summary contains pronouns, we perform pronoun resolution in the source documents using the coreference resolution system by Martschat (2013). If pronoun and antecedent occur in the same sentence, we leave the pronoun. If the antecedent occurs in an earlier sentence, we replace the pronoun in the summary by the first element of the coreference chain the pronoun belongs to. Except for setting λ_1 and λ_2 on DUC 2005, our approach is unsupervised, as there is no traning data required. The recall (ROUGE) scores on different datasets are shown in Table 3.

Table 3 shows that our system would have performed very well in the DUC 2005 and DUC 2006 competitions with ranks in the top 3 and well in the DUC 2007 competition. Since the competitions date a while back, we compare in addition to the current state-of-art in multi-document summarization. To our knowledge Galanis et al. (2012) report the best results on DUC 2005 data. While their ROUGE-2 score is slightly better than ours, we outperform them in terms of ROUGE-SU4 (0.14105 vs. 0.13640), where, to our knowledge, our results are the highest reported so far. However, their results on DUC 2007 (ROUGE-2 0.12517 and ROUGE-SU4 0.17603) are still quite a bit better than our results. On the DUC 2006 data we outperform the HIERSUM system by Haghighi and Vanderwende (2009) on ROUGE-2 (0.08969 vs. 0.086) as well as on ROUGE-SU4 (0.15070 vs. 0.143). On the DUC 2007 data, our results are worse than theirs on ROUGE-2 (0.10928 vs. 0.118) and on par on ROUGE-SU4 (0.16735 vs. 0.167). The system which won the DUC 2007 task, PYTHY by Toutanova et al. (2007), performs similar to HIERSUM and hence slightly better than our system on these data. The recent work by Suzuki and Fukumoto (2014) evaluates also on DUC 2007 but reports only ROUGE-1 scores. We obtain a ROUGE-1 score of 0.448 on DUC 2007 which is better than Suzuki and Fukumoto (2014) (0.438) as well as PYTHY (0.426). The best ROUGE-1 score reported to date has been reported by Celikyilmaz and Hakkani-Tür (2010) with 0.456. The difference between this score and our score of 0.448 is rather small.

5 Discussion

Several approaches have been proposed for topic based multi-document summarization on the DUC datasets we use for our experiments. The best results to date have been obtained by supervised and semi-supervised systems. The results of our system are mostly on par with these systems though our system is unsupervised (as mentioned in Section 4 the values for λ_1 and λ_2 in the objective function (Equation 3) were not tuned for optimal ROUGE scores but rather set for favoring importance over non-redundancy).

We compared our results with various state-of-

[2]Gurobi Optimization, Inc., http://www.gurobi.com

S_1 What is being learned from the study of deep water, seabeds, and deep water life?

S_2 What equipment and techniques are used?

S_3 What are plans for future related activity?

Figure 4: Topic containing interrogative words from DUC 2007

S_1 I've started to use irrigation hoses called "leaky pipe".

S_2 Soil's usually best to water the target area a few days before I plan to dig.

S_3 If I don't place element in the root zone , element can't be added later when the plants are growing.

S_4 The new composts were much lighter and more suitable for container plants in garden centres and through these were rapidly introduced to gardeners.

Figure 5: Sentences containing dangling first person pronoun from DUC 2005

the-art systems, and our system is giving competitive results in both ROUGE-2 and ROUGE-SU4 scores. However, the ROUGE-2 score of Galanis et al. (2012) on DUC 2005 is slightly better than our score. This might be because they use bigram information for redundancy reduction. However, they need training data for sentence importance. Hence their system has to be classified as supervised while ours is unsupervised.

We have also calculated the ROUGE-1 score on DUC 2007 and compared it with state-of-the-art approaches. HybHsum (Celikyilmaz and Hakkani-Tür, 2010) has obtained the top ROUGE-1 score on DUC 2007 with 0.456. However, HybHsum is a semi-supervised approach which requires a labeled training data. The difference between our ROUGE-1 score of 0.448 and HybHsum ROUGE-1 score on DUC2007 is not significant (to be fair, achieving significant improvements in ROUGE scores on DUC data is very difficult). In contrast to HybHsum, our approach is unsupervised.

Our method computes importance on the basis of a bipartite graph. We believe that our bipartite graph captures more information than the general graphs used in earlier graph-based approaches to automatic summarization. Entity transition information present in the bipartite graph of a document, helps us in finding the salient sentences. Our approach works well if the graph is not sparse.

We observed a couple of problems in the output of our system which we plan to address in future work. If topics contain interrogative pronouns as shown in Figure 4 the mapping between topic and sentences from the documents does not work well. We need to resolve which entities the interrogative pronouns refer to. Another problem occurs, because the coreference resolution system employed does not resolve first person pronouns. Hence, we end up with summaries containing dangling first person pronouns as shown in Figure 5. However, our system appears to work reasonably well in other cases where the summaries are coherent and readable and also have a high ROUGE score as shown in the summary from DUC 2007 data in Figure 6.

6 Conclusions

In this paper, we have presented an unsupervised graph based approach for topic based multi-document summarization. Our graph based approach provides state-of-the-art results on various datasets taken from DUC competitions. The graph based representation of a document makes computation very efficient and less complex. In future work, we incorporate the syntactic roles of entities, to provide more information in the method.

Acknowledgments

This work has been funded by Klaus Tschira Foundation, Heidelberg, Germany. The first author has been supported by a Heidelberg Institute for Theoretical Studies Ph.D. scholarship.

The European Parliament , angered by Turkey 's human rights record , voted Thursday to freeze hundreds of millions of US dollars in aid to Turkey for setting up a customs union with the EU. Since then , the EU has been trying to patch up the relationship , with several leaders of member countries insisting that Turkey 's place is in the union. The special aid is part of the agreement between the European Union EU and Turkey on the establishment of a customs union between the two sides. " The European Union , without renouncing its principles , " will have to decide in December to allow Turkey to become a formal candidate for EU membership. ANKARA , February 27 Xinhua Turkey today welcomed the European Union 's attitude toward its dispute with Greece and urged the EU to release financial assistance immediately despite Greek efforts to block it. After the decision in December to exclude Turkey from the first wave of enlargement talks , Turkey put its relations with the 15 member union on hold. During Solana stay here , Turkish leaders reiterated their position to link the expansion of the NATO with Turkey 's entry into the European Union. The European Union , European Union Ankara wants to join , is pressing Turkey to find a peaceful solution to the war. The statement added that Greece , despite its attempts , was unable to get the support of the other 14 European Union members in getting a statement that would express solidarity with Greece and condemn Turkey. Both the European Union and the United States criticized Turkey for jailing Birdal.

Figure 6: Output summary from DUC 2007

Acknowledgments

This work has been funded by Klaus Tschira Foundation, Heidelberg, Germany. The first author has been supported by a Heidelberg Institute for Theoretical Studies Ph.D. scholarship.

References

Regina Barzilay and Michael Elhadad. 1999. Using lexical chains for text summarization. In Inderjeet Mani and Mark T. Maybury, editors, *Advances in Automatic Text Summarization*, pages 111–121. Cambridge, Mass.: MIT Press.

Regina Barzilay and Mirella Lapata. 2008. Modeling local coherence: An entity-based approach. *Computational Linguistics*, 34(1):1–34.

Taylor Berg-Kirkpatrick, Dan Gillick, and Dan Klein. 2011. Jointly learning to extract and compress. In *Proceedings of the 49th Annual Meeting of the Association for Computational Linguistics,* Portland, Oreg., 19–24 June 2011, pages 481–490.

Sergey Brin and Lawrence Page. 1998. The anatomy of a large-scale hypertextual web search engine. *Computer Networks and ISDN Systems*, 30(1–7):107–117.

Jaime G. Carbonell and Jade Goldstein. 1998. The use of MMR, diversity-based reranking for reordering documents and producing summaries. In *Proceedings of the 21st Annual International ACM-SIGIR Conference on Research and Development in Information Retrieval,* Melbourne, Australia, 24–28 August 1998, pages 335–336.

Asli Celikyilmaz and Dilek Hakkani-Tür. 2010. A hybrid hierarchical model for multi-document summarization. In *Proceedings of the 48th Annual Meeting of the Association for Computational Linguistics,* Uppsala, Sweden, 11–16 July 2010, pages 815–824.

Hoa Trang Dang. 2005. Overview of DUC 2005. In *Proceedings of the 2005 Document Understanding Conference held at the Human Language Technology Conference and Conference on Empirical Methods in Natural Language Processing,* Vancouver, B.C., Canada, 9–10 October 2005.

Hoa Trang Dang. 2006. Overview of DUC 2006. In *Proceedings of the 2006 Document Understanding Conference held at the Human Language Technology Conference of the North American Chapter of the Association for Computational Linguistics,* New York, N.Y., 8–9 June 2006.

Micha Elsner and Eugene Charniak. 2011. Extending the entity grid with entity-specific features. In *Proceedings of the ACL 2011 Conference Short Papers,* Portland, Oreg., 19–24 June 2011, pages 125–129.

Güneş Erkan and Dragomir R. Radev. 2004. LexRank: Graph-based lexical centrality as salience in text summarization. *Journal of Artificial Intelligence Research*, 22:457–479.

Mohamed Abdel Fattah and Fuji Ren. 2009. GA, MR, FFNN, PNN and GMM based models for automatic text summarization. *Computer Speech and Language*, 23(1):126–144.

Dimitrios Galanis, Gerasimos Lampouras, and Ion Androutsopoulos. 2012. Extractive multi-document summarization with integer linear programming and support vector regression. In *Proceedings of the 24th International Conference on Computational Linguistics,* Mumbai, India, 8–15 December 2012, pages 911–926.

Daniel Gillick, Korbinian Riedhammer, Benoit Favre, and Dilek Hakkani-Tür. 2009. A global optimization framework for meeting summarization. In *Proceedings of the 2009 IEEE International Conference on Acoustics, Speech, and Signal Processing,* Taipei, Taiwan, 19–24 June 2009, pages 4769–4772.

Jade Goldstein, Vibhu Mittal, Jaime Carbonell, and Mark Kantrowitz. 2000. Multi-document summarization by sentence extraction. In *Proceedings of the Workshop on Automatic Summarization at ANLP/NAACL 2000,* Seattle, Wash., 30 April 2000, pages 40–48.

Yihong Gong and Xin Liu. 2001. Generic text summarization using relevance measure and latent semantic analysis. In *Proceedings of the 24th Annual International ACM SIGIR Conference on Research and Development in Information Retrieval* New Orleans, Louis., 9–12 September 2001, pages 19–25.

Camille Guinaudeau and Michael Strube. 2013. Graph-based local coherence modeling. In *Proceedings of the 51st Annual Meeting of the Association for Computational Linguistics,* Sofia, Bulgaria, 4–9 August 2013, pages 93–103.

Aria Haghighi and Lucy Vanderwende. 2009. Exploring content models for multi-document summarization. In *Proceedings of Human Language Technologies 2009: The Conference of the North American Chapter of the Association for Computational Linguistics,* Boulder, Col., 31 May – 5 June 2009, pages 362–370.

Kai Hong and Ani Nenkova. 2014. Improving the estimation of word importance for news multi-document summarization. In *Proceedings of the 14th Conference of the European Chapter of the Association for Computational Linguistics,* Gothenburg, Sweden, 26–30 April 2014, pages 712–721.

Dan Klein and Christopher D. Manning. 2003. Accurate unlexicalized parsing. In *Proceedings of the 41st Annual Meeting of the Association for Computational Linguistics,* Sapporo, Japan, 7–12 July 2003, pages 423–430.

Jon M. Kleinberg. 1999. Authoritative sources in a hyperlinked environment. *Journal of the ACM,* 46(5):604–632.

Chin-Yew Lin and Eduard Hovy. 2000. The automated acquisition of topic signatures for automatic summarization. In *Proceedings of the 18th International Conference on Computational Linguistics,* Saarbrücken, Germany, 31 July – 4 August 2000, pages 495–501.

Chin-Yew Lin. 2004. ROUGE: A package for automatic evaluation of summaries. In *Proceedings of the Text Summarization Branches Out Workshop at ACL '04,* Barcelona, Spain, 25–26 July 2004, pages 74–81.

H.P. Luhn. 1958. The automatic creation of literature abstracts. *IBM Journal of Research and Development,* 2:159–165.

Sebastian Martschat. 2013. Multigraph clustering for unsupervised coreference resolution. In *Proceedings of the Student Research Workshop at the 51st Annual Meeting of the Association for Computational Linguistics,* Sofia, Bulgaria, 5–7 August 2013, pages 81–88.

Ryan McDonald. 2007. A study of global inference algorithms in multi-document summarization. In *Proceedings of the European Conference on Information Retrieval,* Rome, Italy, 2-5 April 2007.

Kathleen R. McKeown, Judith L. Klavans, Vassileios Hatzivassiloglou, Regina Barzilay, and Eleazar Eskin. 1999. Towards multidocument summarization by reformulation: Progress and prospects. In *Proceedings of the 16th National Conference on Artificial Intelligence,* Orlando, Flo., 18–22 July 1999, pages 453–460.

Rada Mihalcea and Paul Tarau. 2004. TextRank: Bringing order into texts. In *Proceedings of the 2004 Conference on Empirical Methods in Natural Language Processing,* Barcelona, Spain, 25–26 July 2004, pages 404–411.

Rada Mihalcea. 2004. Graph-based ranking algorithms for sentence extraction, applied to text summarization. In *Companion Volume to the Proceedings of the 42nd Annual Meeting of the Association for Computational Linguistics,* Barcelona, Spain, 21–26 July 2004, pages 170–173.

Ani Nenkova and Lucy Vanderwende. 2005. The impact of frequency on summarization. Technical Report MSR-TR-2005-101, Microsoft Research.

Hitoshi Nishikawa, Takaaki Hasegawa, Yoshihiro Matsuo, and Genichiro Kikui. 2010. Opinion summarization with integer linear programming formulation for sentence extraction and ordering. In *Proceedings of the 23rd International Conference on Computational Linguistics,* Beijing, China, 23–27 August 2010, pages 910–918.

Dou Shen, Jian-Tao Sun, Hua Li, Qiang Yang, and Zheng Chen. 2007. Document summarization using conditional random fields. In *Proceedings of the 20th International Joint Conference on Artificial Intelligence,* Hyderabad, India, 6–12 January 2007, pages 2862–2867.

Yoshimi Suzuki and Fumiyo Fukumoto. 2014. Detection of topic and its extrinsic evaluation through multi-document summarization. In *Proceedings of the ACL 2014 Conference Short Papers,* Baltimore, Md., 22–27 June 2014, pages 241–246.

Kristina Toutanova, Chris Brockett, Michael Gamon, Jagadeesh Jagarlamudi, Hisami Suzuki, and Lucy Vanderwende. 2007. The PYTHY summarization system: Microsoft Research at DUC 2007.

In *Proceedings of the 2007 Document Understanding Conference held at the Human Language Technology Conference of the North American Chapter of the Association for Computational Linguistics,* Rochester, N.Y., 26–27 April 2007.

Kristian Woodsend and Mirella Lapata. 2012. Multiple aspect summarization using integer linear programming. In *Proceedings of the 2012 Conference on Empirical Methods in Natural Language Processing and Natural Language Learning,* Jeju Island, Korea, 12–14 July 2012, pages 233–242.

Wen-tau Yih, Joshua Goodman, Lucy Vanderwende, and Hisami Suzuki. 2007. Multi-document summarization by maximizing informative content-words. In *Proceedings of the 20th International Joint Conference on Artificial Intelligence,* Hyderabad, India, 6–12 January 2007, pages 1776–1782.

A Novel Two-stage Framework for Extracting Opinionated Sentences from News Articles

Pujari Rajkumar[1], Swara Desai[2], Niloy Ganguly[1] and Pawan Goyal[1]
[1]Dept. of Computer Science and Engineering,
Indian Institute of Technology Kharagpur, India – 721302
[2]Yahoo! India
[1]rajkumarsaikorian@gmail.com, {niloy,pawang}@cse.iitkgp.ernet.in
[2]swara@yahoo-inc.com

Abstract

This paper presents a novel two-stage framework to extract opinionated sentences from a given news article. In the first stage, Naïve Bayes classifier by utilizing the local features assigns a score to each sentence - the score signifies the probability of the sentence to be opinionated. In the second stage, we use this prior within the HITS (Hyperlink-Induced Topic Search) schema to exploit the global structure of the article and relation between the sentences. In the HITS schema, the opinionated sentences are treated as Hubs and the facts around these opinions are treated as the Authorities. The algorithm is implemented and evaluated against a set of manually marked data. We show that using HITS significantly improves the precision over the baseline Naïve Bayes classifier. We also argue that the proposed method actually discovers the underlying structure of the article, thus extracting various opinions, grouped with supporting facts as well as other supporting opinions from the article.

1 Introduction

With the advertising based revenues becoming the main source of revenue, finding novel ways to increase focussed user engagement has become an important research topic. A typical problem faced by web publishing houses like Yahoo!, is understanding the nature of the comments posted by readers of 10^5 articles posted at any moment on its website. A lot of users engage in discussions in the comments section of the articles. Each user has a different perspective and thus comments in that genre - this many a times, results in a situation where the discussions in the comment section wander far away from the articles topic. In order to assist users to discuss relevant points in the comments section, a possible methodology can be to generate questions from the article's content that seek user's opinions about various opinions conveyed in the article (Rokhlenko and Szpektor, 2013). It would also direct the users into thinking about a spectrum of various points that the article covers and encourage users to share their unique, personal, daily-life experience in events relevant to the article. This would thus provide a broader view point for readers as well as perspective questions can be created thus catering to users with rich user generated content, this in turn can increase user engagement on the article pages. Generating such questions manually for huge volume of articles is very difficult. However, if one could identify the main opinionated sentences within the article, it will be much easier for an editor to generate certain questions around these. Otherwise, the sentences themselves may also serve as the points for discussion by the users.

Hence, in this paper we discuss a two-stage algorithm which picks opinionated sentences from the articles. The algorithm assumes an underlying structure for an article, that is, each opinionated sentence is supported by a few factual statements that justify the opinion. We use the HITS schema to exploit this underlying structure and pick opinionated sentences from the article.

The main contribtutions of this papers are as follows. First, we present a novel two-stage framework for extracting opinionated sentences from a news article. Secondly, we propose a new evaluation metric that takes into account the fact that since the amount of polarity (and thus, the number of opinionated sentences) within documents can vary a lot and thus, we should stress on the ratio of opinionated sentences in the top sentences, relative to the ratio of opinionated sentences in the article. Finally, discussions on how the proposed algorithm captures the underlying structure of the opinions and surrounding facts in a news article reveal that the algorithm does much more than just extracting opinionated sentences.

This paper has been organised as follows. Section 2 discusses related work in this field. In section 3, we discuss our two-stage model in further details. Section 4 discusses the experimental framework and the results. Further discussions on the underlying assumption behind using HITS along with error analysis are carried out in Section 5. Conclusions and future work are detailed in Section 6.

2 Related Work

Opinion mining has drawn a lot of attention in recent years. Research works have focused on mining opinions from various information sources such as blogs (Conrad and Schilder, 2007; Harb et al., 2008), product reviews (Hu and Liu, 2004; Qadir, 2009; Dave et al., 2003), news articles (Kim and Hovy, 2006; Hu and Liu, 2006) etc. Various aspects in opinion mining have been explored over the years (Ku et al., 2006). One important dimension is to identify the opinion holders as well as opinion targets. (Lu, 2010) used dependency parser to identify the opinion holders and targets in Chinese news text. (Choi et al., 2005) use Conditional Random Fields to identify the sources of opinions from the sentences. (Kobayashi et al., 2005) propose a learning based anaphora resolution technique to extract the opinion tuple $< Subject, Attribute, Value >$. Opinion summarization has been another important aspect (Kim et al., 2013).

A lot of research work has been done for opinion mining from product reviews where most of the text is opinion-rich. Opinion mining from news articles, however, poses its own challenges because in contrast with the product reviews, not all parts of news articles present opinions (Balahur et al., 2013) and thus finding opinionated sentences itself remains a major obstacle. Our work mainly focus on classifying a sentence in a news article as opinionated or factual. There have been works on sentiment classification (Wiebe and Riloff, 2005) but the task of finding opinionated sentences is different from finding sentiments, because sentiments mainly convey the emotions and not the opinions. There has been research on finding opinionated sentences from various information sources. Some of these works utilize a dictionary-based (Fei et al., 2012) or regular pattern based (Brun, 2012) approach to identify aspects in the sentences. (Kim and Hovy, 2006) utilize the presence of a single strong valence wors as well as the total valence score of all words in a sentence to identify opinion-bearing sentences. (Zhai et al., 2011) work on finding 'evaluative' sentences in online discussions. They exploit the inter-relationship of aspects, evaluation words and emotion words to reinforce each other.

Thus, while ours is not the first attempt at opinion extraction from news articles, to the best of our knowledge, none of the previous works has exploited the global structure of a news article to classify a sentence as opinionated/factual. Though summarization algorithms (Erkan and Radev, 2004; Goyal et al., 2013) utilize the similarity between sentences in an article to find the important sentences, our formulation is different in that we conceptualize two different kinds of nodes in a document, as opposed to the summarization algorithms, which treat all the sentences equally.

In the next section, we describe the propsoed two-stage algorithm in detail.

3 Our Approach

Figure 1 gives a flowchart of the proposed two-stage method for extracting opinionated sentences from news articles. First, each news article is pre-processed to get the dependency parse as well as the TF-IDF vector corresponding to each of the sentences present in the article. Then, various features are extracted from these sentences which are used as input to the Naïve Bayes classifier, as will be described in Section 3.1. The Naïve Bayes classifier, which corresponds to the first-stage of our method, assigns a probability score to each sentence as being an opinionated sentence. In the second stage, the entire article is viewed as a complete and directed graph with edges from every sentence to all other sentences, each edge having a weight suitably computed. Iterative HITS algorithm is applied to the sentence graph, with opinionated sentences conceptualized as hubs and factual sentences conceptualized as authorities. The two stages of our approach are detailed below.

3.1 Naïve Bayes Classifier

The Naïve Bayes classifier assigns the probability for each sentence being opinionated. The classifier is trained on 70 News articles from politics domain, sentences of which were marked by a group of annotators as being opinionated or factual. Each sentence was marked by two annotators. The inter-annotator agreement using Cohen's kappa coefficient was found to be 0.71.

The features utilized for the classifier are detailed in Table 1. These features were adapted from those reported in (Qadir, 2009; Yu and Hatzivassiloglou, 2003). A list of positive and negative polar words, further expanded using wordnet synsets was taken from (Kim and Hovy, 2005). Stanford dependency parser (De Marneffe et al., 2006) was utilized to compute the dependencies for each sentence within the news article.

After the features are extracted from the sentences, we used the Weka implementation of Naïve Bayes to train the classifier[1].

Table 1: Features List for the Naïve Bayes Classifier

1.	Count of positive polar words
2.	Count of negative polar words
3.	Polarity of the root verb of the sentence
4.	Presence of aComp, xComp and advMod dependencies in the sentence

3.2 HITS

The Naïve Bayes classifier as discussed in Section 3.1 utilizes only the local features within a sentence. Thus, the probability that a sentence is opinionated remains

[1] http://www.cs.waikato.ac.nz/ml/weka/

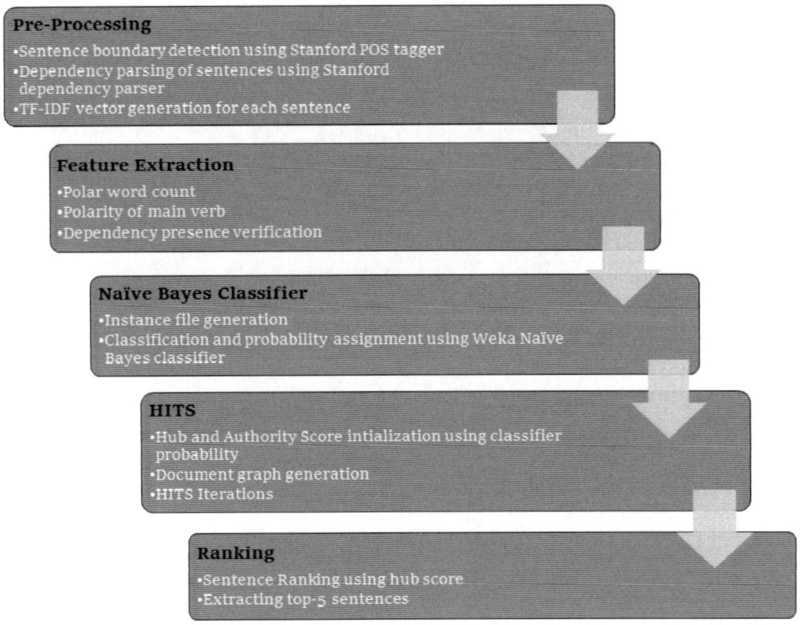

Figure 1: Flow Chart of Various Stages in Our Approach

independent of its context as well as the document structure. The main motivation behind formulating this problem in HITS schema is to utilize the hidden link structures among sentences. HITS stands for 'Hyperlink-Induced Topic Search'; Originally, this algorithm was developed to rank Web-pages, with a particular insight that some of the webpages (**Hubs**) served as catalog of information, that could lead users directly to the other pages, which actually contained the information (**Authorities**).

The intuition behind applying HITS for the task of opinion extraction came from the following assumption about underlying structure of an article. A news article pertains to a specific theme and with that theme in mind, the author presents certain opinions. These opinions are justified with the facts present in the article itself. We conceptualize the opinionated sentences as **Hubs** and the associated facts for an opinionated sentence as **Authorities** for this **Hub**.

To describe the formulation of HITS parameters, let us give the notations. Let us denote a document D using a set of sentences $\{S_1, S_2, \ldots, S_i, \ldots, S_n\}$, where n corresponds to the number of sentences in the document D. We construct the sentence graph where nodes in the graph correspond to the sentences in the document. Let H_i and A_i denote the hub and authority scores for sentence S_i. In HITS, the edges always flow from a Hub to an Authority. In the original HITS algorithm, each edge is given the same weight. However, it has been reported that using weights in HITS update improves the performance significantly (Li et al., 2002). In our formulation, since each node has a non-zero probablility of acting as a hub as well as an authority, we have outgoing as well as incoming edges for every node. Therefore, the weights are assigned, keeping in mind the proximity between sentences as well as the probability (of being opinionated/factual) assigned by the classifier. The following criteria were used for deciding the weight function.

- An edge in the HITS graph goes from a hub (source node) to an authority (target node). So, the edge weight from a source node to a target node should be higher if the source node has a high hub score.
- A fact corresponding to an opinionated sentence should be discussing the same topic. So, the edge weight should be higher if the sentences are more similar.
- It is more probable that the facts around an opinion appear closer to that opinionated sentence in the article. So, the edge weight from a source to target node decreases as the distance between the two sentences increases.

Let W be the weight matrix such that W_{ij} denotes the weight for the edge from the sentence S_i to the sentence S_j. Based on the criteria outlined above, we formulate that the weight W_{ij} should be such that

$$W_{ij} \propto H_i$$
$$W_{ij} \propto Sim_{ij}$$
$$W_{ij} \propto \frac{1}{dist_{ij}}$$

where we use *cosine similarity* between the sentence vectors to compute Sim_{ij}. $dist_{ij}$ is simply the number of sentences separating the source and target node. Various combinations of these factors were tried and will be discussed in section 4. While factors like sentence similarity and distance are symmetric, having the weight function depend on the hub score makes it asymmetric, consistent with the basic idea of HITS. Thus, an edge from the sentence S_i to S_j is given a high weight if S_i has a high probability score of being opinionated (i.e., acting as hub) as obtained the classifier.

Now, for applying the HITS algorithm iteratively, the Hubs and Authorities scores for each sentence are initialized using the probability scores assigned by the classifier. That is, if $P_i(Opinion)$ denotes the probability that S_i is an opinionated sentence as per the Naïve Bayes Classifier, $H_i(0)$ is initialized to $P_i(Opinion)$ and $A_i(0)$ is initialized to $1 - P_i(Opinion)$. The iterative HITS is then applied as follows:

$$H_i(k) = \Sigma_j W_{ij} A_i(k-1) \quad (1)$$

$$A_i(k) = \Sigma_j W_{ji} H_i(k-1) \quad (2)$$

where $H_i(k)$ denote the hub score for the ith sentence during the kth iteration of HITS. The iteration is stopped once the mean squared error between the Hub and Authority values at two different iterations is less than a threshold ϵ. After the HITS iteration is over, five sentences having the highest Hub scores are returned by the system.

4 Experimental Framework and Results

The experiment was conducted with 90 news articles in politics domain from Yahoo! website. The sentences in the articles were marked as opinionated or factual by a group of annotators. In the training set, 1393 out of 3142 sentences were found to be opinianated. In the test set, 347 out of 830 sentences were marked as opinionated. Out of these 90 articles, 70 articles were used for training the Naïve Bayes classifier as well as for tuning various parameters. The rest 20 articles were used for testing. The evaluation was done in an Information Retrieval setting. That is, the system returns the sentences in a decreasing order of their score (or probability in the case of Naïve Bayes) as being opinionated. We then utilize the human judgements (provided by the annotators) to compute precision at various points. Let $op(.)$ be a binary function for a given rank such that $op(r) = 1$ if the sentence returned as rank r is opinionated as per the human judgements.

A $P@k$ precision is calculated as follows:

$$P@k = \frac{\sum_{r=1}^{k} op(r)}{k} \quad (3)$$

While the precision at various points indicates how reliable the results returned by the system are, it does not take into account the fact that some of the documents are opinion-rich and some are not. For the opinion-rich documents, a high $P@k$ value might be similar to picking sentences randomly, whereas for the documents with a very few opinions, even a lower $P@k$ value might be useful. We, therefore, devise another evaluation metric $M@k$ that indicates the ratio of opinionated sentences at any point, normalized with respect to the ratio of opinionated sentences in the article.

Correspondingly, an $M@k$ value is calculated as

$$M@k = \frac{P@k}{Ratio_{op}} \quad (4)$$

where $Ratio_{op}$ denotes the fraction of opinionated sentences in the whole article. Thus

$$Ratio_{op} = \frac{\text{Number of opinionated sentences}}{\text{Number of sentences}} \quad (5)$$

The parameters that we needed to fix for the HITS algorithm were the weight function W_{ij} and the threshold ϵ at which we stop the iteration. We varied ϵ from 0.0001 to 0.1 multiplying it by 10 in each step. The results were not sensitive to the value of ϵ and we used $\epsilon = 0.01$. For fixing the weight function, we tried out various combinations using the criteria outlined in Section 3.2. Various weight functions and the corresponding $P@5$ and $M@5$ scores are shown in Table 2. Firstly, we varied k in ${Sim_{ij}}^k$ and found that the square of the similarity function gives better results. Then, keeping it constant, we varied l in ${H_i}^l$ and found the best results for $l = 3$. Then, keeping both of these constants, we varied α in $(\alpha + \frac{1}{d})$. We found the best results for $\alpha = 1.0$. With this α, we tried to vary l again but it only reduced the final score. Therefore, we fixed the weight function to be

$$W_{ij} = {H_i}^3(0){Sim_{ij}}^2(1 + \frac{1}{dist_{ij}}) \quad (6)$$

Note that $H_i(0)$ in Equation 6 corresponds to the probablity assigned by the classifier that the sentence S_i is opinionated.

We use the classifier results as the baseline for the comparisons. The second-stage HITS algorithm is then applied and we compare the performance with respect to the classifier. Table 3 shows the comparison results for various precision scores for the classifier and the HITS algorithm. In practical situation, an editor requires quick identification of 3-5 opinionated sentences from the article, which she can then use to formulate questions. We thus report $P@k$ and $M@k$ values for $k = 3$ and $k = 5$.

From the results shown in Table 3, it is clear that applying the second-stage HITS over the Naïve Bayes Classifier improves the performance by a large degree, both in term of $P@k$ and $M@k$. For instance, the first-stage NB Classifier gives a $P@5$ of 0.52 and $P@3$ of 0.53. Using the classifier outputs during the second-stage HITS algorithm improves the

Table 2: Average $P@5$ and $M@5$ scores: Performance comparison between various functions for W_{ij}

Function	$P@5$	$M@5$
Sim_{ij}	0.48	0.94
Sim_{ij}^2	0.57	1.16
Sim_{ij}^3	0.53	1.11
$Sim_{ij}^2 H_i$	0.6	1.22
$Sim_{ij}^2 H_i{}^2$	0.61	1.27
$Sim_{ij}^2 H_i{}^3$	0.61	1.27
$Sim_{ij}^2 H_i{}^4$	0.58	1.21
$Sim_{ij}^2 H_i{}^3 \frac{1}{d}$	0.56	1.20
$Sim_{ij}^2 H_i{}^3(0.2 + \frac{1}{d})$	0.60	1.25
$Sim_{ij}^2 H_i{}^3(0.4 + \frac{1}{d})$	0.61	1.27
$Sim_{ij}^2 H_i{}^3(0.6 + \frac{1}{d})$	0.62	1.31
$Sim_{ij}^2 H_i{}^3(0.8 + \frac{1}{d})$	0.62	1.31
$Sim_{ij}^2 H_i{}^3(1 + \frac{1}{d})$	**0.63**	**1.33**
$Sim_{ij}^2 H_i{}^3(1.2 + \frac{1}{d})$	0.61	1.28
$Sim_{ij}^2 H_i{}^2(1 + \frac{1}{d})$	0.6	1.23

Table 3: Average $P@5$, $M@5$, $P@3$ and $M@3$ scores: Performance comparison between the NB classifier and HITS

System	P@5	M@5	P@3	M@3
NB Classifier	0.52	1.13	0.53	1.17
HITS	0.63	1.33	0.72	1.53
Imp. (%)	**+21.2**	**+17.7**	**+35.8**	**+30.8**

preformance by 21.2% to 0.63 in the case of $P@5$. For $P@3$, the improvements were much more significant and a 35.8% improvement was obtained over the NB classifier. $M@5$ and $M@3$ scores also improve by 17.7% and 30.8% respectively.

Strikingly, while the classifier gave nearly the same scores for $P@k$ and $M@k$ for $k = 3$ and $k = 5$, HITS gave much better results for $k = 3$ than $k = 5$. Specially, the $P@3$ and $M@3$ scores obtained by HITS were very encouraging, indicating that the proposed approach helps in pushing the opinionated sentences to the top. This clearly shows the advantage of using the global structure of the document in contrast with the features extracted from the sentence itself, ignoring the context.

Figures 2 and 3 show the $P@5$, $M@5$, $P@3$ and $M@3$ scores for individual documents as numbered from 1 to 20 on the X-axis. The articles are sorted as per the ratio of $P@5$ (and $M@5$) obtained using the HITS and NB classifier. Y-axis shows the corresponding scores. Two different lines are used to represent the results as returned by the classifier and the HITS algorithm. A dashed line denotes the scores obtained by HITS while a continuous line denotes the scores obtained by the NB classifier. A detailed analysis of these figures can help us draw the following conclusions:

- For 40% of the articles (numbered 13 to 20) HITS improves over the baseline NB classifier. For 40% of the articles (numbered 5 to 12) the results provided by HITS were the same as that of the baseline. For 20% of the articles (numbered 1 to 4) HITS gives a performance lower than that of the baseline. Thus, for 80% of the documents, the second-stage performs at least as good as the first stage. This indicates that the second-stage HITS is quite robust.
- $M@5$ results are much more robust for the HITS, with 75% of the documents having an $M@5$ score > 1. An $M@k$ score > 1 indicates that the ratio of opinionated sentences in top k sentences, picked up by the algorithm, is higher than the overall ratio in the article.
- For 45% of the articles, (numbered 6, $9 - 11$ and $15 - 20$), HITS was able to achieve a $P@3 = 1.0$. Thus, for these 9 articles, the top 3 sentences picked up by the algorithm were all marked as opinionated.

The graphs also indicate a high correlation between the results obtained by the NB classifier and HITS. We used Pearson's correlation to find the correlation strength. For the $P@5$ values, the correlation was found to be 0.6021 and for the $M@5$ values, the correlation was obtained as 0.5954.

In the next section, we will first attempt to further analyze the basic assumption behind using HITS, by looking at some actual Hub-Authority structures, captured by the algorithm. We will also take some cases of failure and perform error analysis.

5 Discussion

First point that we wanted to verify was, whether HITS is really capturing the underlying structure of the document. That is, are the sentences identified as authorities for a given hub really correspond to the facts supporting the particular opinion, expressed by the hub sentence.

Figure 4 gives two examples of the Hub-Authority structure, as captured by the HITS algorithm, for two different articles. For each of these examples, we show the sentence identified as Hub in the center along with the top four sentences, identified as Authorities for that hub. We also give the annotations as to whether the sentences were marked as 'opinionated' or 'factual' by the annotators.

In both of these examples, the hubs were actually marked as 'opinionated' by the annotators. Additionally, we find that all the four sentences, identified as authorities to the hub, are very relevant to the opinion expressed by the hub. In the first example, top 3 authority sentences are marked as 'factual' by the annotator. Although the fourth sentence is marked as 'opinionated', it can be seen that this sentence presents a supporting opinion for the hub sentence.

While studying the second example, we found that while the first authority does not present an important fact, the fourth authority surely does. Both of these

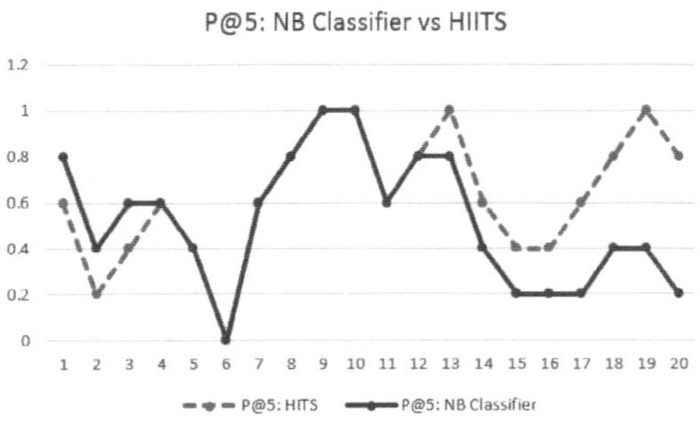

(a) Comparison of P@5 values

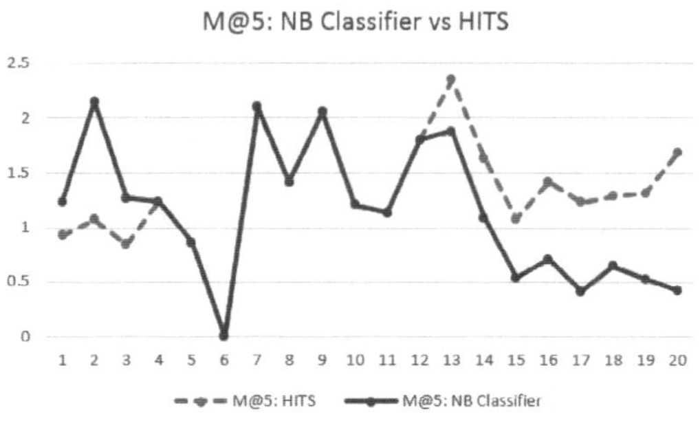

(b) Comparison of M@5 values

Figure 2: Comparison Results for 20 Test articles between the Classifier and HITS: P@5 and M@5

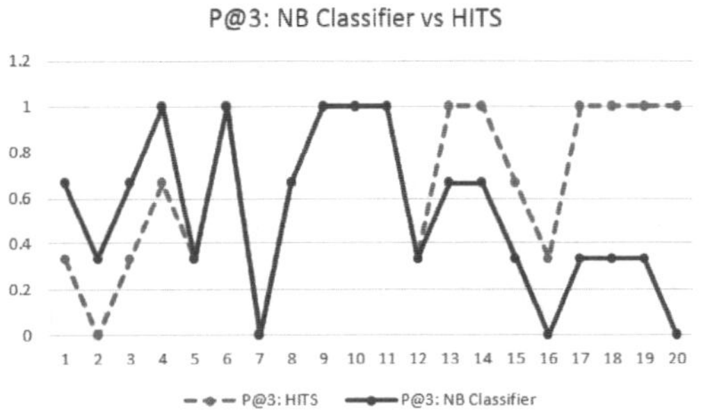

(a) Comparison of P@3 values

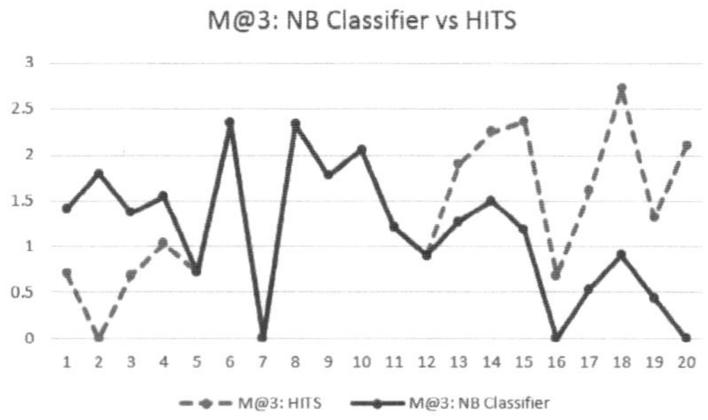

(b) Comparison of M@3 values

Figure 3: Comparison Results for 20 Test articles between the Classifier and HITS: P@3 and M@3

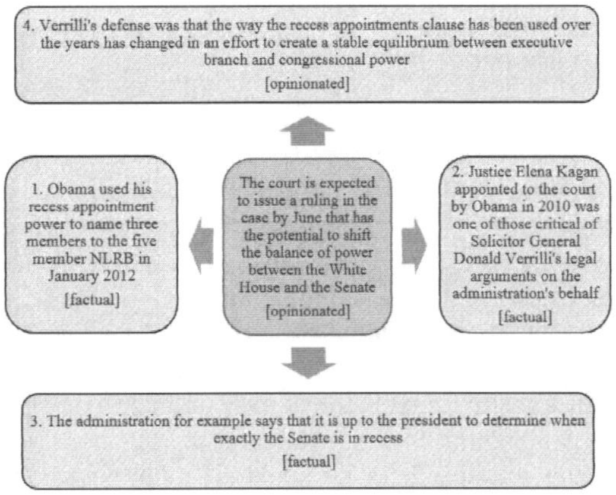

(a) Hub-Authority Structure: Example 1

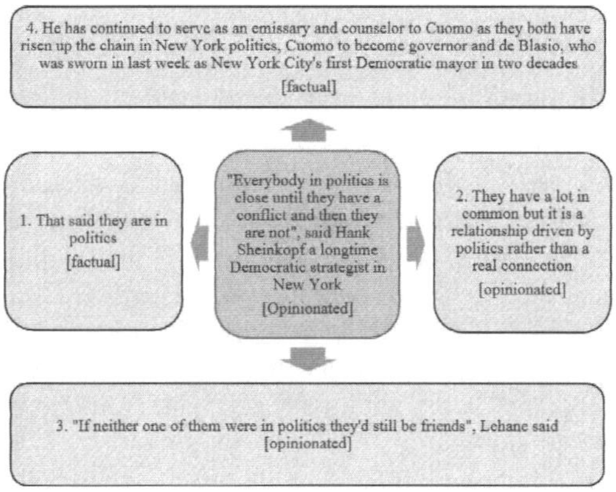

(b) Hub-Authority Structure: Example 2

Figure 4: Example from two different test articles capturing the Hub-Authority Structure

were marked as 'factual' by the annotators. In this particular example, although the second and third authority sentences were annotated as 'opinionated', these can be seen as supporting the opinion expressed by the hub sentence. This example also gives us an interesting idea to improve diversification in the final results. That is, once an opinionated sentence is identified by the algorithm, the hub score of all its suthorities can be reduced proportional to the edge weight. This will reduce the chances of the supporting opinions being reurned by the system, at a later stage as a main opinion.

We then attempted to test our tool on a recently published article, **"What's Wrong with a Meritocracy Rug?"**[2]. The tool could pick up a very

[2]http://news.yahoo.com/whats-wrong-meritocracy-rug-070000354.html

important opinion in the article, "*Most people tend to think that the most qualified person is someone who looks just like them, only younger.*", which was ranked 2nd by the system. The supporting facts and opinions for this sentence, as discovered by the algorithm were also quite relevant. For instance, the top two authorities corresponding to this sentence hub were:

1. *And that appreciation, we learned painfully, can easily be tinged with all kinds of gendered elements without the person who is making the decisions even realizing it.*
2. *And many of the traits we value, and how we value them, also end up being laden with gender overtones.*

5.1 Error Analysis

We then tried to analyze certain cases of failures. Firstly, we wanted to understand why HITS was not performing as good as the classifier for 3 articles (Figures 2 and 3). The analysis revealed that the supporting sentences for the opinionated sentences, extracted by the classifier, were not very similar on the textual level. Thus a low cosine similarity score resulted in having lower edge weights, thereby getting a lower hub score after applying HITS. For one of the articles, the sentence picked up by HITS was wrongly annotated as a factual sentence.

Then, we looked at one case of failure due to the error introduced by the classifier prior probablities. For instance, the sentence, "*The civil war between establishment and tea party Republicans* ***intensified*** *this week when House Speaker John Boehner slammed outside* ***conservative*** *groups for* ***ridiculous*** *pushback against the bipartisan budget agreement which cleared his chamber Thursday.*" was classified as an opinionanted sentence, whereas this is a factual sentence. Looking closely, we found that the sentence contains three polar words (marked in bold), as well as an $advMod$ dependency between the pair (slammed,when). Thus the sentence got a high initial prior by the classifier. As a result, the outgoing edges from this node got a higher ${H_i}^3$ factor. Some of the authorities identified for this sentence were:

- *For Democrats, the tea party is the gift that keeps on giving.*
- *Tea party sympathetic organizations, Boehner later said, "are pushing our members in places where they don't want to be".*

which had words, similar to the original sentence, thus having a higher Sim_{ij} factor as well. We found that these sentences were also very close within the article. Thus, a high hub prior along with a high outgoing weight gave rise to this sentence having a high hub score after the HITS iterations.

5.2 Online Interface

To facilitate easy usage and understanding of the system by others, a web interface has been built for the system[3]. The webpage caters for users to either input a new article in form of text to get top opinionated sentences or view the output analysis of the system over manually marked test data consisting of 20 articles.

The words in green color are positive polar words, red indicates negative polar words. Words marked in violet are the root verbs of the sentences. The colored graph shows top ranked opinionated sentences in yellow box along with top supporting factual sentences for that particluar opinionated sentence in purple boxes. Snapshots from the online interface are provided in Figures 5 and 6.

6 Conclusions and Future Work

In this paper, we presented a novel two-stage framework for extracting the opinionated sentences in the news articles. The problem of identifying top opinionated sentences from news articles is very challenging, especially because the opinions are not as explicit in a news article as in a discussion forum. It was also evident from the inter-annotator agreement and the kappa coefficient was found to be 0.71.

The experiments conducted over 90 News articles (70 for training and 20 for testing) clearly indicate that the proposed two-stage method almost always improves the performance of the baseline classifier-based approach. Specifically, the improvements are much higher for $P@3$ and $M@3$ scores (35.8% and 30.8% over the NB classifier). An $M@3$ score of 1.5 and $P@3$ score of 0.72 indicates that the proposed method was able to push the opinionated sentences to the top. On an average, 2 out of top 3 sentences returned by the system were actually opinionated. This is very much desired in a practical scenario, where an editor requires quick identification of 3-5 opinionated sentences, which she can then use to formulate questions.

The examples discussed in Section 5 bring out another important aspect of the proposed algorithm. In addition to the main objective of extracting the opinionated sentences within the article, the proposed method actually discovers the underlying structure of the article and would certainly be useful to present various opinions, grouped with supporting facts as well as supporting opinions in the article.

While the initial results are encouraging, there is scope for improvement. We saw that the results obtained via HITS were highly correlated with the Naïve Bayes classifier results, which were used in assigning a weight to the document graph. One direction for the future work would be to experiment with other features to improve the precision of the classifier. Additionally, in the current evaluation, we are not evaluating the degree of diversity of the opinions returned by the system. The Hub-Authority

[3]available at `http://cse.iitkgp.ac.in/resgrp/cnerg/temp2/final.php`

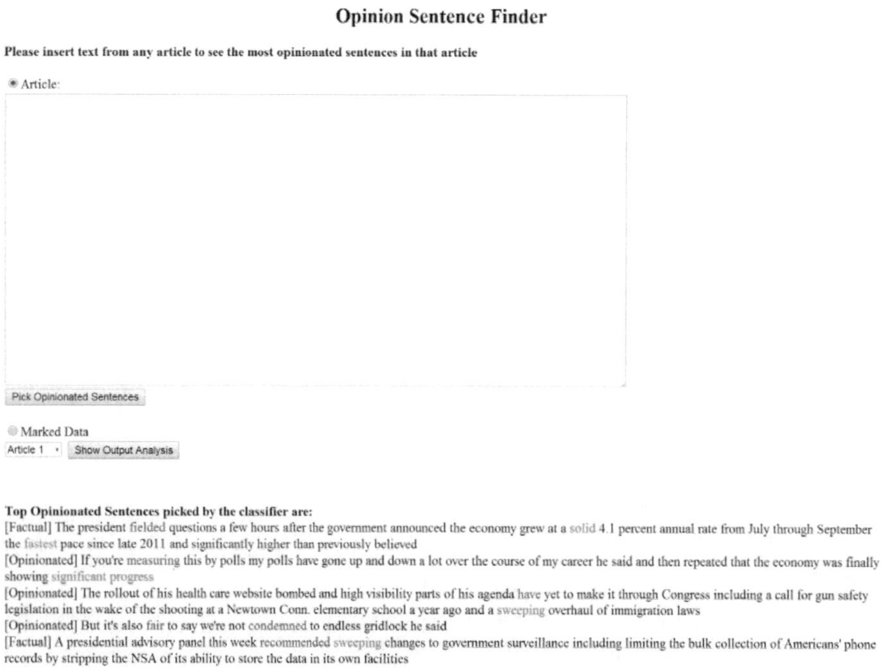

Figure 5: Screenshot from the Web Interface

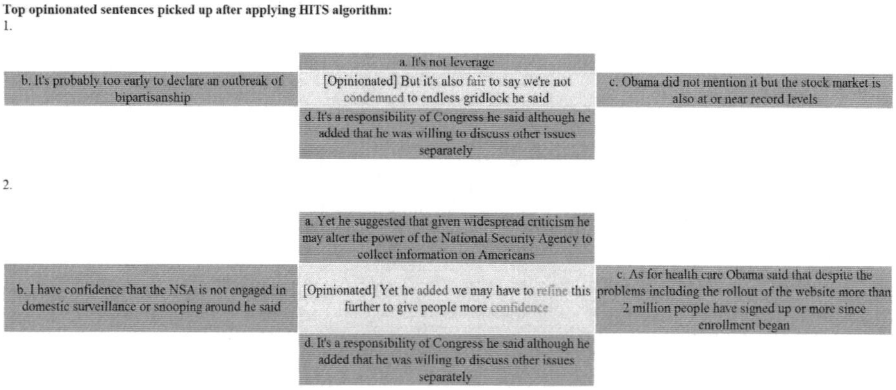

Figure 6: Hub-Authority Structure as output on the Web Interface

structure of the second example gives us an interesting idea to improve diversification and we would like to implement that in future.

In the future, we would also like to apply this work to track an event over time, based on the opinionated sentences present in the articles. When an event occurs, articles start out with more factual sentences. Over time, opinions start surfacing on the event, and as the event matures, opinions predominate the facts in the articles. For example, a set of articles on a plane crash would start out as factual, and would offer expert opinions over time. This work can be used to plot the maturity of the media coverage by keeping track of facts v/s opinions on any event, and this can be used by organizations to provide a timeline for the event. We would also like to experiment with this model on a different media like microblogs.

References

Alexandra Balahur, Ralf Steinberger, Mijail Kabadjov, Vanni Zavarella, Erik Van Der Goot, Matina Halkia, Bruno Pouliquen, and Jenya Belyaeva. 2013. Sentiment analysis in the news. *arXiv preprint arXiv:1309.6202*.

Caroline Brun. 2012. Learning opinionated patterns for contextual opinion detection. In *COLING (Posters)*, pages 165–174.

Yejin Choi, Claire Cardie, Ellen Riloff, and Siddharth Patwardhan. 2005. Identifying sources of opinions with conditional random fields and extraction patterns. In *Proceedings of the conference on Human Language Technology and Empirical Methods in Natural Language Processing*, pages 355–362. Association for Computational Linguistics.

Jack G Conrad and Frank Schilder. 2007. Opinion mining in legal blogs. In *Proceedings of the 11th international conference on Artificial intelligence and law*, pages 231–236. ACM.

Kushal Dave, Steve Lawrence, and David M Pennock. 2003. Mining the peanut gallery: Opinion extraction and semantic classification of product reviews. In *Proceedings of the 12th international conference on World Wide Web*, pages 519–528. ACM.

Marie-Catherine De Marneffe, Bill MacCartney, Christopher D Manning, et al. 2006. Generating typed dependency parses from phrase structure parses. In *Proceedings of LREC*, volume 6, pages 449–454.

Günes Erkan and Dragomir R Radev. 2004. Lexrank: Graph-based lexical centrality as salience in text summarization. *J. Artif. Intell. Res.(JAIR)*, 22(1):457–479.

Geli Fei, Bing Liu, Meichun Hsu, Malu Castellanos, and Riddhiman Ghosh. 2012. A dictionary-based approach to identifying aspects im-plied by adjectives for opinion mining. In *Proceedings of COLING 2012 (Posters)*.

Pawan Goyal, Laxmidhar Behera, and Thomas Martin McGinnity. 2013. A context-based word indexing model for document summarization. *Knowledge and Data Engineering, IEEE Transactions on*, 25(8):1693–1705.

Ali Harb, Michel Plantié, Gerard Dray, Mathieu Roche, François Trousset, and Pascal Poncelet. 2008. Web opinion mining: How to extract opinions from blogs? In *Proceedings of the 5th international conference on Soft computing as transdisciplinary science and technology*, pages 211–217. ACM.

Minqing Hu and Bing Liu. 2004. Mining opinion features in customer reviews. In *Proceedings of Nineteeth National Conference on Artificial Intellgience (AAAI)*.

Minqing Hu and Bing Liu. 2006. Opinion extraction and summarization on the web. In *AAAI*, volume 7, pages 1621–1624.

Soo-Min Kim and Eduard Hovy. 2005. Automatic detection of opinion bearing words and sentences. In *Proceedings of IJCNLP*, volume 5.

Soo-Min Kim and Eduard Hovy. 2006. Extracting opinions, opinion holders, and topics expressed in online news media text. In *Proceedings of the Workshop on Sentiment and Subjectivity in Text*, pages 1–8. Association for Computational Linguistics.

Hyun Duk Kim, Malu Castellanos, Meichun Hsu, ChengXiang Zhai, Umeshwar Dayal, and Riddhiman Ghosh. 2013. Compact explanatory opinion summarization. In *Proceedings of the 22nd ACM international conference on Conference on information & knowledge management*, pages 1697–1702. ACM.

Nozomi Kobayashi, Ryu Iida, Kentaro Inui, and Yuji Matsumoto. 2005. Opinion extraction using a learning-based anaphora resolution technique. In *The Second International Joint Conference on Natural Language Processing (IJCNLP), Companion Volume to the Proceeding of Conference including Posters/Demos and Tutorial Abstracts*.

Lun-Wei Ku, Yu-Ting Liang, and Hsin-Hsi Chen. 2006. Opinion extraction, summarization and tracking in news and blog corpora. In *AAAI Spring Symposium: Computational Approaches to Analyzing Weblogs*, volume 100107.

Longzhuang Li, Yi Shang, and Wei Zhang. 2002. Improvement of hits-based algorithms on web documents. In *Proceedings of the 11th international conference on World Wide Web*, pages 527–535. ACM.

Bin Lu. 2010. Identifying opinion holders and targets with dependency parser in chinese news texts. In *Proceedings of Human Language Technologies: The 2010 Annual Conference of the North American Chapter of the ACL*.

Ashequl Qadir. 2009. Detecting opinion sentences specific to product features in customer reviews using typed dependency relations. In *Proceedings of the Workshop on Events in Emerging Text Types*, eETTs '09, pages 38–43.

Oleg Rokhlenko and Idan Szpektor. 2013. Generating synthetic comparable questions for news articles. In *ACL*, pages 742–751.

Janyce Wiebe and Ellen Riloff. 2005. Creating subjective and objective sentence classifiers from unannotated texts. In *Computational Linguistics and Intelligent Text Processing*, pages 486–497. Springer.

Hong Yu and Vasileios Hatzivassiloglou. 2003. Towards answering opinion questions: Separating facts from opinions and identifying the polarity of opinion sentences. In *Proceedings of the 2003 Conference on Empirical Methods in Natural Language Processing*, EMNLP '03, pages 129–136.

Zhongwu Zhai, Bing Liu, Lei Zhang, Hua Xu, and Peifa Jia. 2011. Identifying evaluative sentences in online discussions. In *Proceedings of the Twenty-Fifth AAAI Conference on Artificial Intelligence*.

Constructing Coherent Event Hierarchies from News Stories

Goran Glavaš and **Jan Šnajder**
University of Zagreb, Faculty of Electrical Engineering and Computing
Text Analysis and Knowledge Engineering Lab
Unska 3, 10000 Zagreb, Croatia
{goran.glavas, jan.snajder}@fer.hr

Abstract

News describe real-world events of varying granularity, and recognition of internal structure of events is important for automated reasoning over events. We propose an approach for constructing coherent event hierarchies from news by enforcing document-level coherence over pairwise decisions of spatiotemporal containment. Evaluation on a news corpus annotated with event hierarchies shows that enforcing global spatiotemporal coreference of events leads to significant improvements (7.6% F_1-score) in the accuracy of pairwise decisions.

1 Introduction

Although real-world events have exact spatiotemporal extent, event mentions in text are often spatially and temporally vague. Moreover, event mentions typically denote real-world events of varying granularity (e.g., *summit* vs. *conversation*). If not addressed, these issues hinder event-based inference.

Research efforts in event extraction have focused on either extracting temporal relations (Pustejovsky et al., 2003a; UzZaman et al., 2013) or recognizing spatial relations (Mani et al., 2010; Roberts et al., 2013) between events. Apart from being difficult to recognize, temporal and spatial containment – when considered in isolation – do not suffice to infer that one event is a part of another. Temporally, an event may happen *during* another event and not be a part of it, as in (1).

(1) *In the midst of the World* ***War*** *II, the Argentinian government* ***reduced*** *rents.*

In this case, *"the reduction of rents in Argentina"* happened *during "the World War II,"* but was not part of it. Conversely, an event may occur *within* the spatial extent of another event and not be a part of it, as shown by (2).

(2) *The fire* ***destroyed*** *60% of London after almost 30,000 people died from* ***plague***.

The spatial extent of *"destruction by fire"* is contained *within* the extent of *"people dying from plague,"* but the former is not a part of the latter. An event e_1 is a part of event e_2 if and only if e_1 is spatially *and* temporally contained within e_2.

In previous research (Chambers and Jurafsky, 2008; Jans et al., 2012), news narratives were modeled as *chains* of events involving the same participants. Such script-like representations, however, do not account for the non-linear (hierarchical) nature of events. In contrast, in this work we model the structure of events in a narrative via relations of *spatiotemporal containment* (STC) between event mentions, effectively inducing a hierarchy of events. We construct directed acyclic graphs of event mentions, in which edges denote STC relations between events. We call this structure an *event hierarchy directed acyclic graph* (EHDAG).

We propose a two-step approach for constructing EHDAGs from news. We first detect the STC relations between pairs of event mentions in a supervised fashion, building on our previous approach (Glavaš et al., 2014). We then enforce structural coherence over local predictions, framing the task as a constrained optimization problem, which we solve using Integer Linear Programming (ILP).

2 Related Research

Introduction of the TimeML standard (Pustejovsky et al., 2003a) and the TimeBank corpus (Pustejovsky et al., 2003b) triggered a surge of research on extraction of temporal relations, much of which within TempEval campaigns (Verhagen et al., 2010; UzZaman et al., 2013). More recently, following the emergence of the SpatialML standard (Mani et al., 2010), Roberts et al. (2013) have proposed an annotation scheme and the supervised model for extracting spatial relations between events.

The abovementioned approaches, however, do

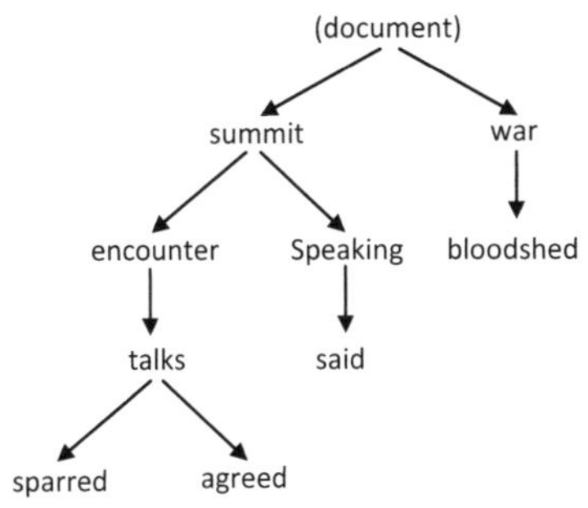

Figure 1: An example of an EHDAG for a narrative

not account for global narrative coherence. Chambers and Jurafsky (2008) consider narratives to be chains of temporally ordered events linked by a common protagonist. Limiting a narrative to a sequence of protagonist-sharing events can often be overly restrictive. E.g., an *"encounter between Merkel and Holland"* may belong to the same "summit" narrative as a *"meeting between Obama and Putin,"* although they share no protagonists.

Several approaches enforce coherence of temporal relations at a document level. Bramsen et al. (2006) represent the temporal structure of a document as a DAG in which vertices denote textual segments and edges temporal precedence. Similarly, Do et al. (2012) enforce coherence using ILP for joint inference on decisions from local event–event and event–time interval decisions.

Complementary to Chambers and Jurafsky (2008), who use a linear temporal structure, with EHDAGs we model the hierarchical structure of events with diverse participants. Similarly to Bramsen et al. (2006), we use an ILP formulation of global coherence over local decisions, but consider STC relations between events rather than temporal relations between textual segments.

3 Constructing Coherent Hierarchies

As an example, consider the following news snippet, with the corresponding EHDAG shown in Fig. 1:

> (3) *Obama* ***sparred*** *with Vladimir Putin over how to end the* ***war*** *in Syria on Monday during an icy* ***encounter*** *at a G8* ***summit. Speaking*** *after* ***talks*** *with Obama, Putin* ***said*** *they* ***agreed*** *the* ***bloodshed*** *must end...*

We first use a supervised classifier to determine the STC relations between all pairs of events in a document. In the second step, we induce a spatiotemporally coherent EHDAG by enforcing coherence constraints on the local classification decisions.

3.1 Spatiotemporal Containment Classifier

We first describe the classifier used for predicting local STC relations. The classifier is given a pair of event mentions, (e_1, e_2), where mention e_1 occurs in text before mention e_2. The classifier predicts one of the following relations: (1) e_1 SUBSUPER e_2, denoting that the e_1 (*subevent*) is spatiotemporally contained by event e_2 (*superevent*); (2) e_1 SUPERSUB e_2, denoting that e_1 (*superevent*) spatiotemporally contains e_2 (*subevent*); and (3) NOREL, denoting that neither of the two events spatiotemporally contains the other. We use the following rich set of features for the STC relation classifier.

Event-based features: Word, lemma, stem, POS-tag, and TimeML type of both event mentions. Additionally, we compare the event arguments of three semantic types: AGENT, TARGET, and LOCATION, which we extract automatically from raw text using the rule-based model by Glavaš and Šnajder (2013).

Bag-of-words features: All lemmas in between the two event mentions, with the special status being assigned to temporal signals (e.g., *before*) and spatial signals (e.g., *inside*).

Positional features: The distance between event mentions in the document, both in the number of sentences and the number of tokens. Additionally, we use a feature indicating if the two mentions are adjacent (no mentions occur in between).

Syntactic features: All dependency relations on the path between events in the dependency tree and features that indicate whether one of the features syntactically governs the other. We compute the syntactic features only for pairs of event mentions from the same sentence, using the Stanford dependency parser (De Marneffe et al., 2006).

Knowledge-based features: Computed using WordNet (Fellbaum, 1998), VerbOcean (Chklovski and Pantel, 2004), and CatVar (Habash and Dorr, 2003). We use a feature indicating whether one event mention or any of its derivatives (obtained from CatVar) is a WordNet hypernym of (for nominalized mentions) or entailed from (for verb mentions) the other mention (or any of its derivatives). We use an additional feature to indicate the VerbOcean relation between the event mentions, if such exists. Unlike features from previous groups, knowledge-based features have not been used often for temporal relation classification.

We employ a L2-regularized logistic regression as our pairwise classification model, which is motivated by the high-dimensional feature space spanned by the lexical features Moreover, the global coherence component of the model requires probability distributions for local decisions over relation types. We use the LibLinear (Fan et al., 2008) implementation of logistic regression.

3.2 Global Coherence

The hierarchy of events induced from the independent pairwise STC decisions may be globally incoherent. We therefore need to optimize the set of pairwise STC classifications with respect to the set of constraints that enforce global coherence. We perform exact inference using Integer Linear Programming (ILP), an approach that has been proven useful in many NLP applications (Punyakanok et al., 2004; Roth and Yih, 2007; Clarke and Lapata, 2008). We use the *lp_solve*[1] solver to optimize the objective function with respect to the constraints.

Objective function. Let $M = \{e_1, e_2, \ldots, e_n\}$ be the set of all event mentions in the news story and P be the set of all considered pairs of event mentions, $P = \{(e_i, e_j) \mid e_i, e_j \in M, i < j\}$. Let $R = \{\text{SUPERSUB}, \text{SUBSUPER}, \text{NOREL}\}$ be the set of spatiotemporal relation types and let $C(e_i, e_j, r)$ be the probability, produced by the pairwise classifier, of relation r holding between event mentions e_i and e_j. We maximize the sum of local probabilities assigned to all pairs of events (summed over all relation types):

$$\sum_{(e_i,e_j)\in P} \sum_{r \in R} C(e_i, e_j, r) \cdot x_{e_i,e_j,r} \quad (1)$$

where $x_{e_i,e_j,r}$ is a binary indicator variable that takes the value 1 iff the relation of type r is predicted to hold between events e_i and e_j.

Spatiotemporal constraints. The objective function is a subject to two basic constraints: (i) the constraint that declares $x_{e_i,e_j,r}$ to be binary indicator variables (eq. 2) and (ii) the exclusivity constraint, which allows only one relation to hold between two events (eq. 3).

$$x_{e_i,e_j,r} \in \{0,1\}, \quad \forall (e_i, e_j) \in P, \; r \in R \quad (2)$$

$$\sum_{r \in R} x_{e_i,e_j,r} = 1, \quad \forall (e_i, e_j) \in P \quad (3)$$

[1] `http://lpsolve.sourceforge.net/5.5/`

Following the work of Bramsen et al. (2006) and Do et al. (2012), we also incorporate the transitivity constraints into the model (transitivity is not enforced for NOREL):

$$x_{e_i,e_j,r} + x_{e_j,e_k,r} - 1 \leq x_{e_i,e_k,r}, \quad (4)$$
$$\forall r \in R, \{(e_i, e_j), (e_j, e_k), (e_i, e_k)\} \subseteq P$$

The transitivity constraint states that, if the same relation r holds for pairs of events (e_i, e_j) and (e_j, e_k), then r must also hold for the pair (e_i, e_k).

Coreference constraints. The constraints presented so far did not consider the coreference of event mentions. However, a truly coherent event structure must account for the different mentions of the same event. More precisely, two different constraints have to be enforced: (i) a pair of coreferent event mentions can only be assigned relation of the NOREL type because coreferent event mentions cannot be part of each other (eq. 5) and (ii) all coreferent mentions of one event must be in the same relation with all coreferent mentions of the other event (eqs. 6–9). Let $\mathit{coref}(e_i, e_j)$ be a predicate that holds iff mentions e_1 and e_2 corefer. The coreference constraints are as follows:

$$x_{e_i,e_j,r} = 1, \quad (5)$$
$$\forall (e_i, e_j) \in P, r = \text{NOREL}, \mathit{coref}(e_i, e_j)$$

$$x_{e_i,e_k,r} - x_{e_j,e_k,r} = 0, \quad (6)$$
$$\forall (e_i, e_k), (e_j, e_k) \in P, r \in R, \mathit{coref}(e_i, e_j)$$

$$x_{e_i,e_k,r} - x_{e_k,e_j,r^{-1}} = 0, \quad (7)$$
$$\forall (e_i, e_k), (e_k, e_j) \in P, r \in R, \mathit{coref}(e_i, e_j)$$

$$x_{e_k,e_i,r} - x_{e_j,e_k,r^{-1}} = 0, \quad (8)$$
$$\forall (e_k, e_i), (e_j, e_k) \in P, r \in R, \mathit{coref}(e_i, e_j)$$

$$x_{e_k,e_i,r} - x_{e_k,e_j,r} = 0, \quad (9)$$
$$\forall (e_k, e_i), (e_k, e_j) \in P, r \in R, \mathit{coref}(e_i, e_j)$$

In equations (7) and (8), the relation type r^{-1} denotes the inverse of the relation type r. The inverse of SUPERSUB is SUBSUPER (and vice versa), whereas NOREL is an inverse to itself.

4 Evaluation

We evaluate several models on the publicly available HIEVE corpus (Glavaš et al., 2014), consisting of 100 news stories manually annotated with event hierarchies.

Model	SUPERSUB P	SUPERSUB R	SUPERSUB F_1	SUBSUPER P	SUBSUPER R	SUBSUPER F_1	Micro-averaged P	Micro-averaged R	Micro-averaged F_1
MEMORIZE baseline	60.3	30.2	40.2	66.8	36.7	47.4	63.8	33.5	43.9
PAIRWISE-NOKB	58.4	47.2	52.2	72.8	**56.2**	63.4	65.5	51.8	57.8
PAIRWISE-FULL	69.8	51.2	59.1	70.6	54.1	61.3	70.2	52.6	60.1
COHERENT	79.6	**60.6**	68.6	73.0	52.0	60.8	76.6	**56.5**	65.0
COREF-AUTO	79.5	57.6	66.8	73.0	52.0	60.8	76.3	55.0	63.9
COREF-GOLD	**87.2**	58.8	**70.3**	**84.2**	52.7	**64.8**	**85.8**	55.9	**67.7**

Table 1: Model performance for recognizing spatiotemporal containment between events

4.1 Experimental Setup

We leave out 20 news stories from the HIEVE corpus for testing and use the remaining 80 documents for training the pairwise STC classifiers. Altogether, we evaluate the following five models.

PAIRWISE model employs only the pairwise classification and does not enforce coherence across local decisions. We evaluate two classifiers: one with knowledge-based features (PAIRWISE-FULL) and one without (PAIRWISE-NOKB).

COHERENT model enforces document-level spatiotemporal coherence by solving the constrained optimization problem on top of pairwise classification decisions. The model uses the constraints from (2)–(4), but not the coreference-based constraints.

COREF-GOLD model uses coreference constraints (6)–(9) in addition to constraints (2)–(4). The model uses hand-annotated coreference relations from the HIEVE corpus.

COREF-AUTO model uses the same set of constraints as the previous model, but relies on the event coreference resolution model by Glavaš and Šnajder (2013) instead on gold annotations.

As the baseline, we use the MEMORIZE model, which simply assigns to each pair of event mentions in the test set their most frequent label in the training set. The NOREL label is predicted for the pairs of lemmas not observed in the training set. A similar baseline has been proposed by Bethard (2008) for automated extraction of event mentions.

To account for the transitivity of the STC relation, we evaluate the predictions of our models against the transitive closure of gold STC hierarchies from the HIEVE corpus.

4.2 Results

Table 1 summarizes the results. We show the performance (precision, recall, and F_1-score) for the SUPERSUB and SUBSUPER relations along with the micro-averaged performance. All models significantly outperform the MEMORIZE baseline (with the exception of PAIRWISE-NOKB's precision), which has been shown competitive on the event extraction task (Bethard, 2008). Overall, the PAIRWISE-FULL model outperforms the PAIRWISE-NOKB model, confirming the intuition that knowledge-based information is useful for detecting relations between events. However, including KB features decreases the performance on the SUBSUPER class, which requires further analysis.

Comparison of the PAIRWISE models and the COHERENT model reveals that enforcing global coherence of local relations substantially improves the quality of the constructed hierarchies (4.9% F_1-score; significant at $p<0.01$ using stratified shuffling (Yeh, 2000)). With the introduction of additional reference constraints (model COREF-GOLD), the quality improves by additional 2.7% F_1-score (significant at $p<0.05$). The fact that the model COREF-AUTO is outperformed by the COHERENT model, however, suggests that the automated coreference resolution model is not accurate enough to benefit the global coherence constraints.

5 Conclusion

We addressed the task of constructing coherent event hierarchies based on recognition of spatiotemporal containment between events from their mentions in text. The proposed approach constructs event hierarchies by enforcing document-level coherence over a set of local decisions on spatiotemporal containment between events. The quality of the extracted event hierarchies is improved by enforcing global coherence, and can be improved even further using event coreference-based constraints, provided accurate coreference resolution is available. Our next step will be to incorporate predictions from state-of-the-art temporal and spatial relation extraction models, both as STC classifier features and as additional optimization constraints.

References

S. Bethard. 2008. *Finding Event, Temporal and Causal Structure in Text: A Machine Learning Approach*. Ph.D. thesis, University of Colorado at Boulder.

P. Bramsen, P. Deshpande, Y. K. Lee, and R. Barzilay. 2006. Inducing temporal graphs. In *Proceedings of the 2006 Conference on Empirical Methods in Natural Language Processing (EMNLP '06)*, pages 189–198. ACL.

N. Chambers and D. Jurafsky. 2008. Unsupervised learning of narrative event chains. In *Proceedings of the 46th Annual Meeting of the Association for Computational Linguistics (ACL 2008)*, pages 789–797.

T. Chklovski and P. Pantel. 2004. VerbOcean: Mining the web for fine-grained semantic verb relations. In *In Proceedings of the 2004 Conference on Empirical Methods in Natural Language Processing (EMNLP '04)*, pages 33–40.

J. Clarke and M. Lapata. 2008. Global inference for sentence compression: An integer linear programming approach. *Journal of Artificial Intelligence Research (JAIR)*, 31:399–429.

M. C. De Marneffe, B. MacCartney, and C. D. Manning. 2006. Generating typed dependency parses from phrase structure parses. In *Proceedings of 5th International Conference on Language Resources and Evaluation (LREC 2006)*, volume 6, pages 449–454.

Q. X. Do, W. Lu, and D. Roth. 2012. Joint inference for event timeline construction. In *Proceedings of the 2012 Joint Conference on Empirical Methods in Natural Language Processing and Computational Natural Language Learning*, pages 677–687. ACL.

R. E. Fan, K. Chang, C. J. Hsieh, X. R. Wang, and C. J. Lin. 2008. LibLinear: A library for large linear classification. *The Journal of Machine Learning Research*, 9:1871–1874.

C. Fellbaum. 1998. *WordNet: An Electronic Lexical Database*. MIT Press.

G. Glavaš and J. Šnajder. 2013. Exploring coreference uncertainty of generically extracted event mentions. In *Proceedings of the Conference in Intelligent Text Processing and Computational Linguistics CICLing 2013*, pages 408–422. Springer.

G. Glavaš, J. Šnajder, P. Kordjamshidi, and M.-F. Moens. 2014. HiEve: A corpus for extracting event hierarchies from news stories. In *Proceedings of 9th Language Resources and Evaluation Conference (LREC 2014)*, pages 3678–3683.

G. Glavaš and J. Šnajder. 2013. Recognizing identical events with graph kernels. In *Proceedings of the 51st Annual Meeting of the Association for Computational Linguistics (ACL 2013)*, pages 797–803. Springer.

N. Habash and B. Dorr. 2003. A categorial variation database for English. In *Proceedings of the 2003 Conference of the North American Chapter of the Association for Computational Linguistics on Human Language Technology-Volume 1*, pages 17–23. ACL.

B. Jans, S. Bethard, I. Vulić, and M. F. Moens. 2012. Skip n-grams and ranking functions for predicting script events. In *Proceedings of the 13th Conference of the European Chapter of the Association for Computational Linguistics*, pages 336–344. ACL.

I. Mani, C. Doran, D. Harris, J. Hitzeman, R. Quimby, J. Richer, B. Wellner, S. Mardis, and S. Clancy. 2010. SpatialML: Annotation scheme, resources, and evaluation. *Language Resources and Evaluation*, 44(3):263–280.

V. Punyakanok, D. Roth, W.-t. Yih, and D. Zimak. 2004. Semantic role labeling via integer linear programming inference. In *Proceedings of the 20th international conference on Computational Linguistics*, page 1346. ACL.

J. Pustejovsky, J. Castano, R. Ingria, R. Sauri, R. Gaizauskas, A. Setzer, G. Katz, and D. Radev. 2003a. TimeML: Robust specification of event and temporal expressions in text. *New Directions in Question Answering*, 3:28–34.

J. Pustejovsky, P. Hanks, R. Sauri, A. See, R. Gaizauskas, A. Setzer, D. Radev, B. Sundheim, D. Day, L. Ferro, et al. 2003b. The TimeBank corpus. In *Corpus Linguistics*, volume 2003, pages 647–656.

K. Roberts, M. A. Skinner, and S. M. Harabagiu. 2013. Recognizing spatial containment relations between event mentions. In *10th International Conference on Computational Semantics*.

D. Roth and W.-t. Yih. 2007. Global inference for entity and relation identification via a linear programming formulation. *Introduction to statistical relational learning*, pages 553–580.

N. UzZaman, H. Llorens, L. Derczynski, M. Verhagen, J. Allen, and J. Pustejovsky. 2013. SemEval-2013 Task 1: TempEval-3: Evaluating time expressions, events, and temporal relations. In *Proceedings of the 7th International Workshop on Semantic Evaluation (SemEval 2013)*. ACL.

M. Verhagen, R. Sauri, T. Caselli, and J. Pustejovsky. 2010. SemEval-2010 Task 13: TempEval-2. In *Proc. of the SemEval 2010*, pages 57–62.

A. Yeh. 2000. More accurate tests for the statistical significance of result differences. In *Proceedings of the 18th conference on Computational linguistics-Volume 2*, pages 947–953. ACL.

Semi-supervised Graph-based Genre Classification for Web Pages

Noushin Rezapour Asheghi
School of Computing
University of Leeds
scs5nra@leeds.ac.uk

Katja Markert
L3S Research Center
Leibniz Universität Hannover
and School of Computing
University of Leeds
markert@l3s.de

Serge Sharoff
School of Modern
Languages and Cultures
University of Leeds
s.sharoff@leeds.ac.uk

Abstract

Until now, it is still unclear which set of features produces the best result in automatic genre classification on the web. Therefore, in the first set of experiments, we compared a wide range of content-based features which are extracted from the data appearing within the web pages. The results show that lexical features such as word unigrams and character n-grams have more discriminative power in genre classification compared to features such as part-of-speech n-grams and text statistics. In a second set of experiments, with the aim of learning from the neighbouring web pages, we investigated the performance of a semi-supervised graph-based model, which is a novel technique in genre classification. The results show that our semi-supervised min-cut algorithm improves the overall genre classification accuracy. However, it seems that some genre classes benefit more from this graph-based model than others.

1 Introduction

In Automatic Genre Identification (AGI), documents are classified based on their genres rather than their topics or subjects. Genre classes such as editorial, interview, news and blog which are recognizable by their distinct purposes, can be on any topic. The most important application of AGI could be in Information Retrieval. If a user could use the search engine to retrieve web pages from a specific genre such as news articles, reviews or blogs, search results could be more beneficial. With the aim of enhancing search engines, AGI has attracted a lot of attention (see Section 2).

In this paper, we investigate two important open questions in AGI. The first question is: what set of features produces the best result in genre classification on the web? The drawbacks of existing genre-annotated web corpora (low inter-coder agreement; false correlations between topic and genre classes) resulted in researchers' doubt on the outcomes of classification models based on these corpora (Sharoff et al., 2010). Therefore, in order to answer this question, we perform genre classification with a wide range of features on a reliable and source diverse genre-annotated web corpus. The second question that we investigate in this paper is: could we exploit the graph structure of the web to increase genre classification accuracy? With the aim of learning from the neighbouring web pages, we investigated the performance of a semi-supervised graph-based model, which is a novel technique in genre classification.

The remainder of this paper is structured as follows. After reviewing related work in Section 2, we compare different supervised genre classification models based on various lexical, POS-based and text statistics features in Section 3. Section 4 describes our semi-supervised graph-based classification experiment, where we use the multi-class min-cut algorithm as a novel technique in genre classification. Section 5 concludes the findings and discusses future work.

2 Related Work

There has been a considerable body of research in AGI. In previous studies on automatic genre classification of web pages, various types of features such as common words (Stamatatos et al., 2000), function words (Argamon et al., 1998), word unigrams (Freund et al., 2006), character n-grams (Kanaris and Stamatatos, 2007), part-of-speech tags (Karlgren and Cutting, 1994) , part-of-speech trigrams (Argamon et al., 1998; Santini, 2007), document statistics (e.g. average sentence length, average word length and type/token ratio) (Finn and Kushmerick, 2006; Kessler et al., 1997), HTML tags (e.g. (Santini, 2007)) have been explored. However, researchers conducted genre classification experiments with different features on different corpora with different sets of genre labels. As a result, it is difficult to compare them. This motivated Sharoff et al. (2010) to examine a wide range of word-based, character-based and POS-based features on the existing genre-annotated corpora. They reported that word unigrams and character 4-grams outperform other features in genre classification. However, they concluded that the results cannot be trusted because of two main reasons. First, some of these collections exhibit low inter-coder agreement and any results based on unreliable data could be misleading. Second, the spurious correlation between topic and genre classes in some of these corpora was one of the reasons for some of the very impressive results reported by Sharoff et al. (2010). These good results were achieved by detecting topics rather than genres of individual texts. A similar point was made by Petrenz and Webber (2010) who examined the impact of topic change on the performance of AGI systems. They showed that a shift in topic can have a massive impact on genre classification models which are based on lexical features such as word unigrams or character n-grams. Therefore, the question which set of features produces the best result in automatic genre classification on the web is still an open question. In order to investigate this question, we perform genre classification with a wide range of features on a reliable and topically diverse dataset. Section 3.1 describes the dataset and the experimental setup.

Most of the current works in the field of AGI concentrated on extracting features from the content of the documents and classify them by employing a standard supervised algorithm. However, on the web there are other sources of information which can be utilized to improve genre classification of web pages. For instance, the web has a graph structure and web pages are connected via hyper-links. These connections could be exploited to improve genre classification. Various graph-based classification algorithms have been proposed to improve topic classification for web pages, such as the relaxation labelling algorithm (Chakrabarti et al., 1998), iterative classification algorithm (Lu and Getoor, 2003), Markov logic networks (Crane and McDowell, 2012), random graph walk (Lin and Cohen, 2010) and weighted-vote relational neighbour algorithm (Macskassy and Provost, 2007). These classification algorithms which utilize hyper-link connections between web pages to construct graphs, outperformed the classifiers which are solely based on textual content of the web pages for topic classification. Such connected data presents opportunities for boosting the performance of genre classification too.

Graph-based web page classification presented in studies such as (Crane and McDowell, 2012; Lu and Getoor, 2003; Macskassy and Provost, 2007) on the WebKB dataset (CRAVEN, 1998) could be considered as genre classification as opposed to topic classification. The WebKB dataset contains web pages from four computer science departments categorised into seven classes: student, faculty, staff, department, course, project and other. However, this dataset is very specific to the academic domain with low coverage for the web overall, whereas we examine graph-based learning for automatic genre classification of web pages on a much more general dataset with popular genre classes such as news, blog and editorial. Moreover, the graph-based algorithms used on the WebKB dataset are all supervised and were performed on a very clean and noise free dataset which was achieved by removing the class other. Class other contains all the web pages which do not belong to any other predefined classes. However, our experiment is in a semi-supervised manner which is a much more realistic scenario on the web, because it is highly unlikely that for each web page, we have genre labels for all its neighbouring web pages as well. Therefore, we perform our experiment on a very noisy dataset where neighbouring web pages could belong to none of our predefined genre classes. Section 4 describes our semi-supervised graph-based classification experiment, where we use a multi-class min-cut algorithm as a novel technique in genre classification.

3 Content-based Classification

3.1 Dataset and Experimental Setup

Petrenz and Webber (2010) and Sharoff et al. (2010) emphasize that the impact of topic on genre classification should be eliminated or controlled. In order to avoid the influence of topic on genre classification, some researchers (e.g. (Sta-

Genre	Number of web pages	Number of websites	# of pages from the same website max	min	med	Fleiss's κ
Personal Homepage (php)	304	288	9	1	1	0.858
Company/ Business Homepage (com)	264	264	1	1	1	0.713
Educational Organization Homepage (edu)	299	299	1	1	1	0.953
Personal Blog /Diary (blog)	244	215	9	1	1	0.812
Online Shop (shop)	292	209	23	1	1	0.830
Instruction/ How to (instruction)	231	142	15	1	1	0.871
Recipe	332	116	8	1	1	0.971
News	330	127	12	1	1	0.801
Editorial	310	69	11	1	3	0.877
Conversational Forum (forum)	280	106	11	1	1	0.951
Biography (bio)	242	190	15	1	1	0.905
Frequently Asked Questions (faq)	201	140	8	1	1	0.915
Review	266	179	15	1	1	0.880
Story	184	24	38	1	7	0.953
Interview	185	154	11	1	1	0.905

Table 1: Statistics for each category illustrate source diversity and reliability of the corpus (Asheghi et al., 2014). To save space, in this paper we use the abbreviation of genre labels which are specified after the genre names.

matatos et al., 2000) and (Argamon et al., 1998)) use only topic independent features such as common words or function words in genre classification. However, neither of these features are exclusive to genre classification. Function words and common words are used in authorship classification (e.g. (Argamon et al., 2007)) because they can capture the style of the authors without being influenced by the topics of the texts. On the other hand, word unigrams are a popular document representation in topic classification. If we want these models to capture the genre of documents without being influenced by their topics or the style of their authors, we must eliminate the influence of these factors on genre classification by keeping them constant across the genre classes in the training data. That means all the documents in the training set should be about the same topic and written by the same person. However, constructing such a dataset is practically impossible for genre classes on the web. The other more practical solution to this problem would be to collect data from various topics and sources in order to minimize the impact of these factors on genre classification. For that reason, we (Asheghi et al., 2014) created a web genre annotated corpus which is reliable (with Fleiss's kappa (Fleiss, 1971) equal to 0.874) and source diverse. We tried to reduce the influence of topic, the writing style of the authors as well as the design of the websites on genre classification by collecting data from various sources and topics. The corpus consists of 3964 web pages from 2522 different websites, distributed across 15 genres (Table 1).

Moreover, we prepared two versions of the corpus: the original text and the main text corpora. First, we converted web pages to plain text by removing HTML markup using the KrdWrd tool (Steger and Stemle, 2009). This resulted in the original text corpus which contains individual web pages with all the textual elements present on them. Moreover, in order to investigate the influence of boilerplate parts (e.g. advertisements, headers, footers, template materials, navigation menus and lists of links) of the web pages on genre classification, we removed the boilerplate parts and extracted the main text of each web page using the justext tool [1]. This resulted in the creation of the main text corpus. This is the first time that the performance of genre classification models is compared on both the original and the main text of the web pages.

Since the outputs of the justext tool for 518 of the web pages were empty files, the main text corpus has fewer pages. However, the main text corpus still has a balanced distribution with a relatively large number of web pages per category. Table 2 compares the number of web pages in the two versions of the corpus. For all the experiments we use this corpus via 10-fold cross-validation on the web pages. Also, in order to minimize the effect of factors such as topic, the writing style of the authors and the design of the websites even further, we ensured that all the web pages from the same website are in the same fold. Many, if not all of the previous studies in automatic genre classification on the web ignored this essential step when dividing the data into folds. For machine learning, we

[1] http://code.google.com/p/justext/

Genre	Number of web pages in corpora	
	Original text	Main text
php	304	221
com	264	190
edu	299	191
blog	244	242
shop	292	221
instruction	231	229
recipe	332	243
news	330	320
editorial	310	307
forum	280	251
bio	242	242
faq	201	160
review	266	262
story	184	184
interview	185	183

Table 2: Number of web pages in individual genre classes in both original text and main text corpora.

chose Support Vector Machines (SVM) because it has been shown by other researchers in AGI (e.g. (Santini, 2007)) that SVM produces better or at least similar results compared to other machine learning algorithms. We used the one-versus-one multi-class SVM implemented in Weka [2] with the default setting. All the experiments are carried out on both the original text and the main text corpora.

3.2 Features

In order to compare the performance of different lexical and structural features used in previous work, we reimplemented the following published approaches to AGI: function words (Argamon et al., 1998), part-of-speech n-grams (Santini, 2007), word unigrams (Freund et al., 2006) and character 4-grams binary representation (Sharoff et al., 2010). We also explored the discriminative power of other features such as readability features (Pitler and Nenkova, 2008), HTML tags [3] and named entity tags in genre classification (Table 3). This is the first time that some of these features such as average depth of syntax trees and entity coherence features (Barzilay and Lapata, 2008) are used for genre classification. To set a base-line, we used a list of genre names (e.g. news, editorial, interview, review) as features. We used two different feature representations: binary and normalized frequency. In the binary representation of a document, the value for each feature is either one or zero which represents the presence or the absence of each feature respectively. In the normalized frequency representation of a document, the value for each feature is the frequency of that feature which is normalized by the length of the document.

For extracting lexical features, we tokenized each document using the Stanford tokenizer (included as part of the Stanford part of speech tagger (Toutanova et al., 2003)) and converted all the tokens to lower case. For extracting POS tags and named entity tags, we used the Stanford maximum entropy tagger [4] and the Stanford Named Entity Recognizer [5] respectively. For extracting some of the readability features such as average parse tree height and average number of noun and verb phrases per sentences, we used the Stanford Parser (Klein and Manning, 2003). However, web pages must be cleaned before they can be fed to a parser, because parsers cannot handle tables and list of links. Therefore, we only used the main text of each web page as an input to the parser. For web pages for which the justext tool produced empty files, we treated these features as missing values. Moreover, we used the Brown Coherence Toolkit [6] to construct the entity grid for each web page and computed the probability of each entity transition type. This tool needs the parsed version of the text as an input. Therefore, for web pages for which the justext tool produced empty files, we also treated these features as missing values.

3.3 Results and Discussion

Table 4 shows the result of the different feature sets listed in the previous section on both the original text and the main text corpora. At first glance, we see that the results of genre classification on the original text corpus are higher than the main text corpus. This shows that boiler plates contain valuable information which helps genre classification.

Moreover, the results show that binary representation of word unigrams is the best performing feature set when we use the whole text of the web pages. However, on the main text corpus, character 4-grams outperform other features. This confirms the results reported in (Sharoff et al., 2010). The results also highlight that the performance of POS-based features are much less accurate than that of textual features such as word unigrams and character n-grams. The results also show that the combination of word unigrams, text statistics and

[2] http://www.cs.waikato.ac.nz/ml/weka/

[3] http://www.w3schools.com/tags/ref_byfunc.asp

[4] http://nlp.stanford.edu/software/tagger.shtml

[5] http://nlp.stanford.edu/software/CRF-NER.shtml

[6] http://www.cs.brown.edu/ melsner/manual.html

Category	Features
Token features	number of tokens and number of types normalized frequency of punctuation marks and currency characters
Named entity tags	normalized frequency of tags: time, location, organization, person, money, date
Readability features	average parse tree height average sentence length and word length standard deviation of sentence length and of word length average number of syllables per word type/token ratio average number of noun phrases and verb phrases per sentence entity coherence features (Barzilay and Lapata, 2008)
HTML tags	normalized frequency of tags for: sections / style, formatting, programming, visual features such as forms, images, lists and tables

Table 3: List of text statistics features explored in this paper

part of speech features resulted in improving genre classification accuracy (compared to the accuracy achieved by word unigrams alone), for both original and main text corpora. However, while the improvement for the main text corpus is statistically significant [7], there is no significant difference between these two models for the original corpus. Surprisingly, adding part of speech 3-grams to the word unigrams features decreased the genre classification accuracy in both original and main text corpora. The reason could be that the model is over-fitted on the training data and as a result, it performs poorly on the test data. Therefore, combining various features will not always improve the performance of the classification task. Moreover, for extracting POS-based features and some of the text statistics features we rely on tools such as part-of-speech taggers and parsers whose performance varies for different genres. Even the best part-of-speech taggers and parsers are error prone and cannot be trusted on new unseen genres.

4 Graph-based Classification

Until now we extracted features only from the content of the web pages. However, other sources of information such as the connections and the link patterns between the web pages could be exploited to improve genre classification. The underlying assumption of this approach is that a page is more likely to be connected to pages with the same genre category. For example, if the neighbouring web pages of a particular web page are labelled as shop, it is more likely that this web page is a shop too, whereas, it is highly unlikely that it is a news or editorial. This property (i.e. entities with similar labels are more likely to be connected) is known as homophily (Sen et al., 2008). We hypothesis that homophily exists for genre classes and it can help us to improve genre classification on the web. In this paper, we use a semi-supervised graph-based algorithm namely, multi-class min-cut, which is a novel approach in genre classification. This algorithm, which is a collective classification method, considers the class labels of all the web pages within a graph.

[7]McNemar test at the significance level of 5%

4.1 Multi-class Min-cut: The Main Idea

The Min-cut classification algorithm originally proposed by Blum and Chawla (2001) is based on the idea that linked entities have a tendency to belong to the same class. In other words, it is based on the homophily assumption. Therefore, it should be able to improve genre classification on the web if our hypothesis holds. However, this technique is a binary classification algorithm, whereas, we have a multi-class problem. Unfortunately, multi-class min-cut is NP-hard and there is no exact solution for it. Nevertheless, Ganchev and Pereira (2007) proposed a multi-class extension to Blum and Chawla (2001)'s min-cut algorithm by encoding a multi-class min-cut problem as an instance of metric labelling. Kleinberg and Tardos (1999; 2002) introduced metric labelling for the first time. The main idea of metric labelling for web page classification can be described as follows:

Assume we have a weighted and undirected graph $G = (V, E)$ where each vertex $v \in V$ is a web page and the edges represent the hyper-links between the web pages. The task is to classify these web pages into a set of labels L. This task can be denoted as a function $f : V \rightarrow L$. In order to do this labelling task in an optimal way, we need to minimize two different types of costs. First, there is a non-negative cost $c(v, l)$ for assigning label l

Feature set	Original text	Main text
genre names bin	57.39	29.02
genre name nf	38.29	14.16
function words bin	65.71	55.57
function words nf	74.95	66.86
word unigrams bin	**89.32**	76.61
word unigrams nf	85.21	74.91
character 4-grams bin	87.96	**78.88**
POS-3grams bin	73.18	61.23
POS-3grams nf	70.28	57.83
POS-2grams bin	64.10	54.91
POS-2grams nf	68.94	60.76
POS nf	60.14	54.64
text statistics	55.47	59.17
word unigrams bin + text statistics	**89.48**	78.09
word uni-grams bin + text statistics + POS nf	**89.63**	78.24
word uni-grams bin + POS 3-grams bin	88.14	75.59

Table 4: Classification accuracy of different features in genre classification. *bin* and *nf* refer to the use of binary and normalized frequency representation of the features respectively.

to web page v. Second, if two web pages v_1 and v_2 are connected together with an edge e with weight w_e, we need to pay a cost of $w_e \cdot d(f(v_1), f(v_2))$ where $d(.,.)$ denotes distance between the two labels. A big distance value between labels indicates less similarity between them. Therefore, the total cost of labelling task f is:

$$E(f) = \sum_{v \in V} c(v, f(v)) + \sum_{e=(v_1,v_2) \in E} w_e \cdot d(f(v_1), f(v_2)) \quad (1)$$

Kleinberg and Tardos (1999; 2002) developed an algorithm for minimizing $E(f)$. However, their algorithm uses linear programming which is impractical for large data (Boykov et al., 2001). In a separate study for metric labelling problems, Boykov et al. (2001) have developed a multi-way min-cut algorithm to minimize $E(f)$. This algorithm is very fast and can be applied to large-scale problems with good performance (Boykov et al., 2001).

4.2 Selection of unlabelled data

A web page w has different kind of neighbours on the web such as parents, children, siblings, grand parents and grand children which are mainly differentiated based on the distance to the target web page as well as the direction of the links (Qi and Davison, 2009). Since the identification of children of a web page (i.e. web pages which have direct links from the target web page) is a straightforward task as their URLs can be extracted from the HTML version of the target web page, in this study, we explore the effect of the target web pages' children on genre classification. Therefore, in this experiment, by neighbouring web pages we mean the web pages' children. In order to collect the neighbouring web pages, for every web page in the data set, we extracted all its out-going URLs and downloaded them as unlabelled data. However, using all these neighbouring pages could hurt the genre classification accuracy because web pages are noisy (e.g. links to advertisements) and some neighbours could have different genres than the target page. In order to control the negative impact of such neighbours, we could preselect a subset of neighbours whose content are close enough to the target page. To implement this idea, we

Cosine similarity	# of unlabelled web pages	Average # of neighbours
≥ 0	103,372	40.65
≥ 0.1	98,824	39.08
≥ 0.2	87,834	34.23
≥ 0.3	70,602	26.46
≥ 0.4	50,232	17.52
≥ 0.5	28,437	8.62
≥ 0.6	13,919	3.77
≥ 0.7	7,241	1.86
$\geq$ 0.8	**3,772**	**0.98**
≥ 0.9	1,732	0.44

Table 5: Number of unlabelled web pages with different cosine similarity thresholds. The last column shows the average number of neighbours per labelled page.

computed the cosine similarity between the web page w and its neighbouring web pages and used different threshold to select the neighbours. If u is a neighbour of w and $\overrightarrow{u}$ and $\overrightarrow{w}$ are the representative feature vectors of these two web pages respectively, we could compute the cosine similarity between these two web pages using the following formula:

$$\cos(\overrightarrow{w}, \overrightarrow{u}) = \frac{\overrightarrow{w} \cdot \overrightarrow{u}}{\| \overrightarrow{w} \| \| \overrightarrow{u} \|} = \frac{\sum_{i=1}^{n} w_i \times u_i}{\sqrt{\sum_{i=1}^{n} (w_i)^2} \times \sqrt{\sum_{i=1}^{n} (u_i)^2} \quad (2)$$

where n is the number of the dimensions of the vectors and w_i is the value of the ith dimension of the vector $\overrightarrow{w}$. Since the word unigrams binary representation model yields the best result for content-based genre classification, we used this representation of web pages to construct their feature vectors. Table 5 shows the number of unlabelled data and the average number of neighbours per labelled web page for different cosine similarity thresholds.

4.3 Formulation of Semi-supervised Multi-class Min-cuts

The formulation of semi-supervised multi-class min-cut for genre classification involves the following steps:

1. We built the weighted and undirected graph $G = (V, E)$ where vertices are the web pages (labelled and unlabelled) and the edges represent the hyper-links between the web pages and set the weights to 1.

2. For training nodes, set the cost of the correct label to zero and all other labels to a large constant.

3. For test nodes and unlabelled nodes, we set the cost of each label using a supervised classifier (SVM) using the following formula:

   $$c(w, l) = 1 - p_l(w) \quad (3)$$

   where $c(w, l)$ is the cost of label l for web page w and $p_l(w)$ is the probability of w belonging to the label l which is computed by a supervised SVM using word unigrams binary representation of the web pages.

4. Set $d(i, j)$, which denotes the distance between two labels i and j, to 1 if $i \neq j$ and zero otherwise.

5. Employ Boykov et al. (2001) algorithm to find the minimum total cost using multiway min-cut algorithm.

4.4 Results and Discussion

We divided the labelled data into 10 folds again ensuring that all the web pages from the same websites are in the same fold. We used 8 folds for training, one fold for validation and one fold for testing. We learnt the best cosine similarity threshold using validation data and then evaluated it on the test data. Tables 6 and 7 illustrate the results of the multi-class min-cut algorithm and the content-based algorithm (both using word unigrams as features) respectively. The results show that the multi-class min-cut algorithm significantly outperforms [8] the content-based classifier for the cosine similarity equal or greater than 0.8 which was chosen on the validation data. It must be noted that the result of the multi-class min-cut algorithm when we used all the neighbouring pages was much lower than the content-based algorithm due to noise. The results also shows that some genre classes such as news, editorial, blog, interview and instruction benefited more than other genre classes from the neighbouring web pages. Genre categories with improved results are shown in bold in Table 6. The homophily property of these genre categories was the reason behind this improvement. For example, the fact that a news article is more likely to be linked to other news articles, whereas, an editorial is more likely to be linked to other editorials, helped us to differentiate these two categories further. On the other hand, we observe no improvement or even decrease in F-measure for some genre categories such as frequently asked questions, forums and company home pages. Two reasons could have contributed to these results. First, the homophily property might not exist for these categories. Second, the homophily property holds for these categories, however, in order to benefit from this property, we need to examine other neighbours of the target web pages such as parents, siblings, grand parents, grand children or even more distant neigh-

[8]McNemar test at the significance level of 5%

class	Recall	Precision	F1-measure
php	**0.928**	**0.850**	**0.887**
forum	0.925	0.977	0.951
review	0.895	0.832	0.862
news	**0.897**	**0.798**	**0.845**
com	0.897	0.891	0.894
shop	**0.860**	**0.965**	**0.910**
instruction	**0.870**	**0.914**	**0.892**
recipe	**0.994**	**0.991**	**0.993**
blog	**0.889**	**0.879**	**0.884**
bio	**0.905**	**0.948**	**0.926**
editorial	**0.800**	**0.932**	**0.861**
faq	0.902	0.841	0.870
edu	**0.957**	**0.963**	**0.960**
story	**0.902**	**0.943**	**0.922**
interview	**0.870**	**0.809**	**0.839**
overall accuracy = **90.11%**			

Table 6: Recall, Precision and F-measure for multi-class min-cut genre classification.

class	Recall	Precision	F1-measure
php	0.938	0.798	0.862
forum	0.943	0.974	0.958
review	0.872	0.859	0.866
news	0.894	0.782	0.835
com	0.920	0.874	0.897
shop	0.849	0.950	0.897
instruction	0.866	0.889	0.877
recipe	0.988	0.988	0.988
blog	0.865	0.841	0.853
bio	0.884	0.926	0.905
editorial	0.765	0.926	0.837
faq	0.866	0.879	0.872
edu	0.950	0.969	0.959
story	0.864	0.941	0.901
interview	0.827	0.785	0.805
overall accuracy = 88.98% [9]			

Table 7: Recall, Precision and F-measure for content-based genre classification using word unigrams feature set

bours.

5 Conclusions and Future work

In the first set of experiments, we compared a diverse range of content-based features in genre classification using a reliable and source diverse genre-annotated corpus. The evaluation shows that lexical features outperformed all other features. Source diversity of the corpus minimized the influence of topic, authorship and web page design on genre classification. In the second experiment, we significantly improved the genre classification result using a semi-supervised min-cut algorithm by employing the children of the target web pages as unlabelled data. The results of this method which takes advantage of the graph structure of the web shows that some genre classes benefit more than others from the neighbouring web pages. The homophily property of genre categories such as news, blogs and editorial was the reason behind the improvement of genre classification in this experiment. In future work, we would like to examine the effect of other types of neighbours on genre classification of web pages and experiment with other graph-based algorithms.

References

Shlomo Argamon, Moshe Koppel, and Galit Avneri. 1998. Routing documents according to style. In *First international workshop on innovative information systems*, pages 85–92. Citeseer.

Shlomo Argamon, Casey Whitelaw, Paul Chase, Sobhan Raj Hota, Navendu Garg, and Shlomo Levitan. 2007. Stylistic text classification using functional lexical features. *Journal of the American Society for Information Science and Technology*, 58(6):802–822.

Noushin Rezapour Asheghi, Serge Sharoff, and Katja Markert. 2014. Designing and evaluating a reliable corpus of web genres via crowd-sourcing. In *Proceedings of the Ninth International Conference on Language Resources and Evaluation (LREC'14)*.

Regina Barzilay and Mirella Lapata. 2008. Modeling local coherence: An entity-based approach. *Computational Linguistics*, 34(1):1–34.

Avrim Blum and Shuchi Chawla. 2001. Learning from labeled and unlabeled data using graph mincuts. In *Proceedings of the Eighteenth International Conference on Machine Learning*, pages 19–26. Morgan Kaufmann Publishers Inc.

Yuri Boykov, Olga Veksler, and Ramin Zabih. 2001. Fast approximate energy minimization via graph cuts. *Pattern Analysis and Machine Intelligence, IEEE Transactions on*, 23(11):1222–1239.

Soumen Chakrabarti, Byron Dom, and Piotr Indyk. 1998. Enhanced hypertext categorization using hyperlinks. In *ACM SIGMOD Record*, volume 27, pages 307–318. ACM.

Robert Crane and Luke McDowell. 2012. Investigating markov logic networks for collective classification. In *ICAART (1)*, pages 5–15.

M CRAVEN. 1998. Learning to extract symbolic knowledge from the world wide web. In *Proc. of the 15th National Conference on Artificial Intelligence (AAAI-98)*.

[9]Please note that in this experiment we had less training data because we used 8 folds for training, one fold for validation and one fold for testing. As a result, the accuracy of word unigrams is slightly lower than the result reported in Table 4.

Aidan Finn and Nicholas Kushmerick. 2006. Learning to classify documents according to genre. *Journal of the American Society for Information Science and Technology*, 57(11):1506–1518.

J.L. Fleiss. 1971. Measuring nominal scale agreement among many raters. *Psychological Bulletin*, 76(5):378.

L. Freund, C.L.A. Clarke, and E.G. Toms. 2006. Towards genre classification for ir in the workplace. In *Proceedings of the 1st international conference on Information interaction in context*, pages 30–36. ACM.

Kuzman Ganchev and Fernando Pereira. 2007. Transductive structured classification through constrained min-cuts. *TextGraphs-2: Graph-Based Algorithms for Natural Language Processing*, page 37.

Ioannis Kanaris and Efstathios Stamatatos. 2007. Webpage genre identification using variable-length character n-grams. In *Tools with Artificial Intelligence, 2007. ICTAI 2007. 19th IEEE International Conference on*, volume 2, pages 3–10. IEEE.

J. Karlgren and D. Cutting. 1994. Recognizing text genres with simple metrics using discriminant analysis. In *Proceedings of the 15th conference on Computational linguistics-Volume 2*, pages 1071–1075.

B. Kessler, G. Numberg, and H. Schutze. 1997. Automatic detection of text genre. In *Proceedings of the 35th Annual Meeting of the Association for Computational Linguistics and Eighth Conference of the European Chapter of the Association for Computational Linguistics*, pages 32–38.

Dan Klein and Christopher D Manning. 2003. Accurate unlexicalized parsing. In *Proceedings of the 41st Annual Meeting on Association for Computational Linguistics-Volume 1*, pages 423–430. Association for Computational Linguistics.

Jon Kleinberg and Eva Tardos. 1999. Approximation algorithms for classification problems with pairwise relationships: Metric labeling and markov random fields. In *focs*, page 14. Published by the IEEE Computer Society.

Jon Kleinberg and Eva Tardos. 2002. Approximation algorithms for classification problems with pairwise relationships: Metric labeling and markov random fields. *Journal of the ACM (JACM)*, 49(5):616–639.

Frank Lin and William W Cohen. 2010. Semi-supervised classification of network data using very few labels. In *Advances in Social Networks Analysis and Mining (ASONAM), 2010 International Conference on*, pages 192–199. IEEE.

Q. Lu and L. Getoor. 2003. Link-based classification using labeled and unlabeled data. *The Continuum from Labeled to Unlabeled Data in Machine Learning & Data Mining*, page 88.

Sofus A Macskassy and Foster Provost. 2007. Classification in networked data: A toolkit and a univariate case study. *The Journal of Machine Learning Research*, 8:935–983.

P. Petrenz and B. Webber. 2010. Stable classification of text genres. *Computational Linguistics*, (Early Access):1–9.

Emily Pitler and Ani Nenkova. 2008. Revisiting readability: A unified framework for predicting text quality. In *Proceedings of the Conference on Empirical Methods in Natural Language Processing*, pages 186–195.

Xiaoguang Qi and Brian D Davison. 2009. Web page classification: Features and algorithms. *ACM Computing Surveys (CSUR)*, 41(2):12.

Marina Santini. 2007. *Automatic identification of genre in web pages*. Ph.D. thesis, University of Brighton.

Prithviraj Sen, Galileo Namata, Mustafa Bilgic, Lise Getoor, Brian Galligher, and Tina Eliassi-Rad. 2008. Collective classification in network data. *AI magazine*, 29(3):93.

S. Sharoff, Z. Wu, and K. Markert. 2010. The web library of babel: evaluating genre collections. In *Proceedings of the Seventh Conference on International Language Resources and Evaluation*, pages 3063–3070.

Efstathios Stamatatos, Nikos Fakotakis, and George Kokkinakis. 2000. Text genre detection using common word frequencies. In *Proceedings of the 18th conference on Computational linguistics-Volume 2*, pages 808–814.

Johannes M. Steger and Egon W. Stemle. 2009. KrdWrd – architecture for unified processing of web content.

Kristina Toutanova, Dan Klein, Christopher D Manning, and Yoram Singer. 2003. Feature-rich part-of-speech tagging with a cyclic dependency network. In *Proceedings of the 2003 Conference of the North American Chapter of the Association for Computational Linguistics on Human Language Technology-Volume 1*, pages 173–180.

The Modular Community Structure of Linguistic Predication Networks

Aaron Gerow
Computation Institute
University of Chicago
Chicago, IL, USA
gerow@uchicago.edu

James Evans
Dept. of Sociology & Computation Institute
University of Chicago
Chicago, IL, USA
jevans@uchicago.edu

Abstract

This paper examines the structure of linguistic predications in English text. Identified by the copular "is-a" form, predications assert category membership (hypernymy) or equivalence (synonymy) between two words. Because predication expresses ontological structure, we hypothesize that networks of predications will form modular groups. To measure this, we introduce a semantically motivated measure of *predication strength* to weight relevant predications observed in text. Results show that predications do indeed form modular structures without any weighting ($Q \approx 0.6$) and that using predication strength increases this modularity ($Q \approx 0.9$) without discarding low-frequency items. This high level of modularity supports the network-based analysis and the use of predication strength as a way to extract dense semantic clusters. Additionally, words' centrality within communities exhibits slight correlation with hypernym depths in WordNet, underscoring the ontological organization of predication.

1 Introduction & Background

Statistical patterns in language use are evident at many levels and have proved useful in an increasingly wide range of computational and cognitive applications. Statistical regularities offer a way to quantify and model how people create, encode and use knowledge about the world. Statements specifically about "what things are" (ie. ontological statements) offer uniquely transparent evidence about peoples' knowledge of the world. Our research adopts a corpus-based approach in which networks of predications are analyzed to assess the underlying structure of ontological assertions.

Word-word predications, observed as the copular `is-a` form in English, are important because, unlike most grammatical constructions that have few semantic constraints, predications tend to imply category membership or equivalence. Take (i) and (ii) for example:

(i) Safety is always a primary concern.
(ii) This organization is an institution where [...].

(i) is a category assertion (*safety* as a type of *concern*) and (ii) is an equivalence assertion (*organization* is an *institution*). Most predications can be interpreted as category memberships like (i); explicit articulation of equivalence is actually quite rare in language (Cimiano, 2006; Cimiano and Völker, 2005). Although some categorical predications are metaphorical, many of these are interpreted using category matching or analogical mapping processes (Glucksberg et al., 1997; Bowdle and Gentner, 2005). In both semantic interpretations, predications naturally form a directed network of words. Consisting primarily of category assertions, the structure of this network should exhibit a degree of natural clustering owing natural categories of the those things it represents.

Network representations of language have been used to describe a wide range of structures in language, including word-word and word-document co-occurrences, term collocations, dependency structure and named entity relations. Networks of grammatical relations have been found to differentiate word-classes (Ferrer i Cancho et al., 2004) and semantic networks can be used to model vocabulary growth (Steyvers and Tenenbaum, 2005). Co-occurrence networks, which are perhaps the most widely studied natural language network, are the foundation of many vector-space models (Landauer and Dumais, 1997; Turney et al., 2010) and can be used to mine synonyms (Cohen et al., 2005), disambiguate word senses (Agirre et al., 2014; Biemann, 2006) and even help mark the quality of essays (Foltz et al., 1999). Spectral methods applied to linguistic networks have been used to differentiate languages (Ferrer i Cancho et al., 2004), word-classes (Sun and Korhonen, 2009) and genres of text (Ferrer i Cancho et al., 2007). Using spectral methods, research has also found that syntactic and semantic distributional similarity networks have considerably different structure (Biemann et al., 2009). The use of lexical graphs (networks of words) in particular, pre-dates modern NLP (Rapoport et al., 1966), though the approach continues to influence a variety of NLP and information retrieval tasks like summarization and retrieval (Erkan and Radev, 2004; Véronis, 2004). Network-based methods have even used community detection, similar to the algorithm described in this paper, tò extract specialist terms from sets of multi-theme documents (Grineva et al., 2009) as well as unstructured texts (Gerow, 2014).

Because predications naturally form directed chains of ontological assertions, we hypothesize that their underlying structure is systematic and modular, given its representation of naturally organized things in the world. Our method employs community detection on networks of noun-noun predications as a way to assess the *overall* structure of predication, but it could be extended to hypernym and category extraction tasks (Hearst, 1992; Caraballo, 1999). Specifically, we test for community structure in predications and explore whether this structure becomes more highly resolved when using a semantic measure of *predication strength* introduced in the following section. We also predict that central nodes (i.e. words) in individual modules will correlate to categorical super-ordinance or hypernymy. Thus, we first seek to assess the *overall* community structure of predication, testing whether or not it is more resolved using a novel measure of *predication strength*. Second, within communities of predications, we compare the words' closeness centrality to their positions in WordNet's hypernym tree (Miller, 1995).

2 Method

Unlike co-occurrence networks, where words are related simply by proximity, predication networks are built using extracted grammatical relationships. The implied relationship in a co-occurrence network provides a natural way to weight edges, but predications have no analogue to a proximity-based weighting scheme. One option would be to weight edges by the number of times given predications were observed. While this is perhaps the most obvious way to account for important predications, it risks exaggerating high-frequency items that are common for reasons other than importance (perhaps they are idioms, collocates or found in abnormally strong colligational structures). Frequency weighting would also be susceptible to noise from the many low-frequency items. To address these concerns, we introduce a semantically informed measure of predication relevance.

Wilks' (1975; 1978) theory of preference semantics proposes that subject- and object-verb relationships evince "selectional preference", which can be thought of as the disposition verbs have to select certain arguments – particular classes of subjects or objects. To operationalize selectional preference, Resnik (1997) introduced *selectional preference strength* to measure the disposition or "preference" of a verb, v:

$$S_R(v) = \sum_{c \in C} P(c|v) \log \frac{P(c|v)}{P(c)} \qquad (1)$$

where C is a set of semantic classes from which v can select and R is the grammatical relation in question. Note that $S_R(v)$ is effectively the sum K-L divergence between the probabilities of v and c for all classes. In a corpus-based setting, the probability of any word can be estimated by its relative frequency: $P(x) = \frac{f(x)}{\sum_i f(x_i)}$. Resnik goes on to define a measure of *selectional association* between a verb and a specific class, c:

$$A_R(v,c) = \frac{1}{S_R(v)} P(c|v) \log \frac{P(c|v)}{P(c)} \qquad (2)$$

In the typical form of selectional preference induction – the task of estimating likelihoods over all classes – Eq. 2 is used to measure a verb's preference for classes of nominal subjects or objects like vehicles, insects, birds, etc. (Resnik, 1997; Shutova et al., 2013).

To test our assumptions regarding the modular structure of predications in English, a measure like selectional association should account for predicates' diversity (or uniformity) of attachment. That is, the preference a predicate has to operate on a wide or narrow range of words. To account for this, we add a term, $U(p)$, to account for the relative number of *unique* words a predicate p has been observed to predicate. Note that this is not the total number of predications involving p, which would produce problematically high values were p to collocate strongly with the words it predicates. Instead, $U(p)$ addresses and normalizes for the diversity with which p is applied. Additionally, instead of using a pre-set collection of semantic classes on which predication is assumed to operate, each predicate is treated as its own class. For a predication consisting of word w predicated by p, predication strength is defined as follows:

$$PS(w,p) = \frac{1}{S_R(p)} \log \frac{P(w|p)}{U(p)P(w)} \qquad (3)$$

PS thus combines three important properties of predications: the relative frequency of a given predication $P(w|p)$, the relative frequency of a word $P(w)$ and the diversity of a word's potential predications $U(p)$. Defined like this, $U(p)$ helps diminish the contribution of predicates that are widely applicable, under the assumption that being widely used, they are in-fact somewhat less significant. Using this measure to weight edges in a predication network should help diminish the contribution of exceptionally frequent predications as well as that from low-frequency predications without excluding them.

An example predication network is shown in Figure 1. In these networks, a network is constructed over a set of documents where nodes are the words in a predication, the direction following the is-a link. Thus, example (i) would result in a link from *safety* to *concern* with weight 1. Were another predication involving *concern* to be observed, another edge would be added from that node. Note that circularities are allowed even though this example is acyclic. To assess predication strength as a relevance function, we compare the community structure of weighted and unweighted networks. The example in Figure 1 shows a sample network (top) and the communities extracted from the unweighted and weighted versions of the same network (middle and bottom). Note the changes in community assignments from the unweighted version to the weighted. In particular, observe the new clusters in the weighted network around *money*, *factor* and *murder*. If our

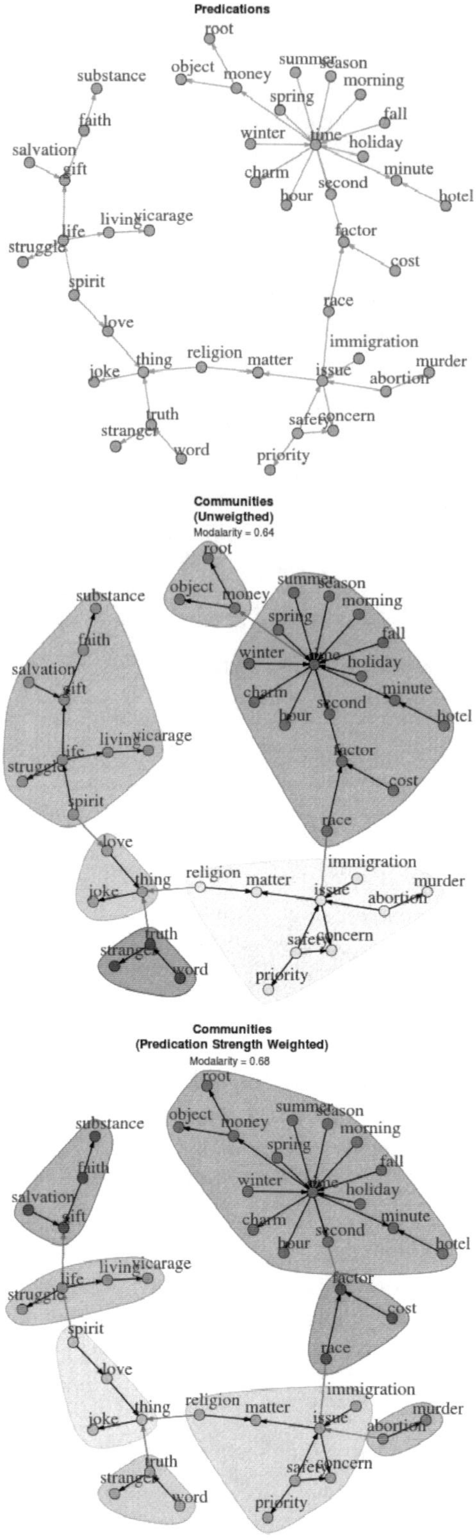

Figure 1: Predication network from the enTenTen corpus (pruned by frequency ≥ 170): the initial network (top), communities assigned by the Infomap algorithm for the unweighted network (middle) and for the network weighted by predication strength (bottom).

intuitions about the systematic nature of linguistic predication is correct, there should be at least a moderate degree of community structure in the unweighted networks, and if predication displays semantic preference similar to selectional association, this community structure should be stronger for networks weighted by predication strength.

The school *librarian* may be the **person** that controls [...]
You may find *Rachel* is the one **person** who may [...]
Neither the state nor its *government* is a **person**.
An *arbitrator* is a **person** who is appointed [...]
On the other hand, an *expert* is a **person** to fix [...]
After all, the *vendor* is the **person** best able to [...]
An *expert* need not be an individual **person**.
The innocent *party* is a natural **person**.
If the *indemnifier* is a natural **person**, [...]
consumers who are natural **persons** under the Directive.

Table 1: Sample predications involving forms of the word *person* as the target in the BNC. In each case an edge would connect the predicate (in italics) to *person* (in bold).

3 Results

To explore the structure of predication networks, we analyzed two corpora using the method described above: the British National Corpus (BNC) (Leech et al., 2001) and the enTenTen web corpus. Predications were extracted templates over a POS-tagged version of each corpus using the Sketch Engine[1] tool (Kilgarriff et al., 2004). The BNC contained about 112 million tokens and the enTenTen collection has 3.2 billion tokens. For each collection, the top 1,000 most frequent nouns provided a seed set from which to extract all `predicate` and `predicate_of` relations[2] (see examples in Table 1). For the BNC, this resulted in 40,721 predications (14,319 unique) and 260,555 (20,651 unique) for the enTenTen collection. Predication strength scores were computed for every predication using within-corpus relative frequencies. These scores were used to weight edges in one version of the predication network, whereas the edge-weights of the "unweighted" version were uniformly set to 1.0. No node-weighting was applied in either case.

[1]http://www.sketchengine.co.uk/

[2]`"NN.?.?" [tag="WP"|tag="PNQ"|tag="CJT"] ?[tag="RB.?"|tag="RB"|tag="VM"]0,5 [lemma="be" & tag="V.*"] "RB.?"0,2 [tag="DT.?"|tag="PP$"]0,1 "CD"0,2 [tag="JJ.?"|tag="RB.?"|word=","]0,3 "NN.?.?"0,2 2:"NN.?.?" [tag!="NN.?.?"]`

Two methods were used to extract communities from the predication networks: the Infomap and walktrap algorithms. By using two methods, we attain some assurance that our findings are not artifacts of the assumptions underlying either algorithm. The Infomap algorithm is an information-theoretic method that exploits the analogue between optimizing a compression dictionary and simplifying a graph by describing "flow" through nodes (Rosvall and Bergstrom, 2008). Infomap assumes edges in a network induce such flow and by deriving a minimum description of this flow, the algorithm can find multi-level communities in large networks (Rosvall and Bergstrom, 2011). The second method, walktrap, operationalizes the intuition that a large set of short random walks on a network will leave walkers on some groups of nodes more often than others (Pons and Latapy, 2005). By setting the walk distance to a small value, relative to a network's density, walkers will tend toward communities if the walker sample is sufficient. These algorithms are both known to work well with large, directed networks and neither imposed intractable computational burdens at our scale (Fortunato, 2010; Lancichinetti and Fortunato, 2009). Because both algorithms require a connected network, our analysis is restricted to the largest connected component (LCC) for all networks, though we have no reason to believe results would differ significantly for other components.

Community assignments can be assessed by measuring how self-contained or "modular" the resulting communities are. Modularity was introduced as a way to choose the level of an optimal cut for hierarchical partitioning algorithms, analogous to the level in the dendrogram that yields the best communities (Newman and Girvan, 2004). For a network with adjacency matrix $\mathbf{A}$ and community assignments c, modularity is defined as:

$$Q = \frac{1}{2m} \sum_{ij} \mathbf{A}_{ij} - \frac{k_i k_j}{2m} \delta(c_i, c_j) \quad (4)$$

where m is the number of edges and k_i is the degree of node i. $\delta(c_i, c_j)$ is 1 when the community assignment of node i is the same as that for node j. Modularity measures how likely it is that nodes in a community are connected to one another as opposed to nodes in other communities. Modularity is defined from -1.0 to 1.0 and graphs where $Q > 0.6$ are conventionally said to have relatively strong community structure (Newman, 2010). Here, we use modularity instead of a measure of semantic similarity or semantic coherence because predication is seldom an assertion of equivalence or similarity. This means that although words in predication communities may be related in an ontological sense, such an assessment would not expose the level of independence between the communities.

Weighted and unweighted networks from both corpora were submitted to each community detection algorithm, the results of which were assessed using modularity. We also carried out this analysis on frequency-weighted networks, the results of which were similar to the unweighted configuration, but are not reported for sake of brevity. Figure 2 shows the modularity for each configuration with varying minimum predication frequency (the number of times a predication had to occur to be included). Varying the minimum frequency thresholds helps simulate the effect of corpus-size on the algorithm. In the BNC, unweighted networks with no minimum edge frequency show slight modularity ($Q = 0.30$), whereas in weighted networks it is quite strong ($Q = 0.89$). The enTenTen corpus exhibits a gap between the unweighted ($Q = 0.61$) and weighted networks ($Q = 0.88$) at low edge thresholds. This shows that predication strength is helpful in weighting relevant items without excluding low-frequency observations. The lower modularity scores (Q; Eq. 4) in the unweighted networks may be due to more novel, loose or figurative associations found in low-frequency predications that inappropriately connect unrelated communities. Interestingly, scores for unweighted and weighted networks converge up to a point as the minimum frequency increases (reducing the size of the network). This pruning is helpful for the unweighted networks, but has little effect on the weighted versions. In all cases, sparsity takes a toll as the LCC becomes quite small. The reason for the eventual decline as the LCC shrinks below 70 nodes is because communities are less likely to form at all in small networks.

In addition to the highly modular structure, the communities of predications themselves are likely to represent some semantic organization. Specifically, we looked for a categorical structure within the communities by comparing words to the hypernym tree in WordNet (Miller, 1995). Intuitively, one would expect words that are central in

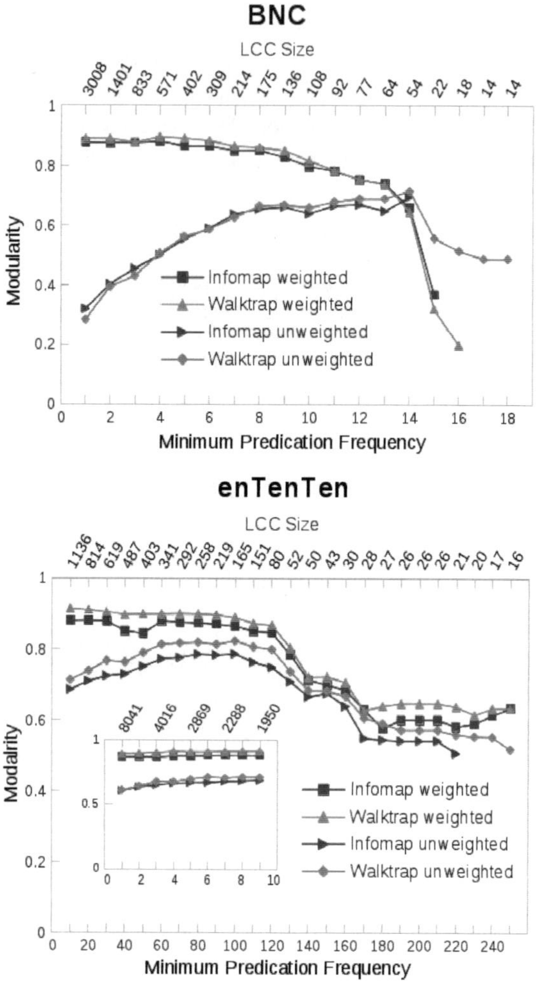

Figure 2: Modularity of predication networks in the BNC (top) and enTenTen (bottom). Note, as the minimum frequency increases (bottom axis) and the LCC contains fewer and fewer nodes (top axis), the community detection algorithms may not produce a solution with more than one community, resulting in undefined modularity.

a community to be members of higher-level categories. In figure 1, for example, *summer*, *hour* and *holiday* all point to *time*, one could infer that *time* is a shared hypernym. We use closeness centrality, a graph-theoretic measure of node's average proximity to other nodes, as a within-community measure of super-ordinance (i.e. hypernymy). Though there a number of network centrality measures, closeness centrality is a robust measure, though it tends not to scale well to larger networks because it requires computing the distance between every pair of nodes (Friedl et al., 2010).

The centrality scores in the communities were compared to WordNet using the first sense-entry for each node (which is typically the most common) and words not found in the tree were discarded. For the unweighted networks across both corpora, we found a mean Spearman correlation of r=0.35 ($p < 0.01$; using Fisher's transformation) for the Infomap algorithm and r=0.38 ($p < 0.01$) for walktrap. In the weighted versions, Infomap produced r=0.41 ($p < 0.01$) and walktrap produced r=0.44 ($p < 0.01$). This confirms that predication communities tend to specify categorical knowledge is moderately similar to WordNet. Note these correlation values are comparable between the weighted and unweighted networks, implying that relevance, as selectional association, is not an important marker of the communities' hypernymic composition.

4 Discussion

The analysis in this paper is an attempt to identify whether or not ontological knowledge expressed in text consists of meaningful clusters. With the network representation and our measure of predication strength, results indicate that predication forms strong community structures. Overall, results point to the highly modular nature of predication, previously unreported in language. This confirms our prediction that predication comprises systematic clusters of related things and the higher modularity observed in networks weighted by predication strength implies that predication exhibits a form of selectional preference. Predication's strong community structure is important because it supports the use of linguistic patterns in establishing ontological representations, which naturally form higher-level groups.

Technically, our measure of predication strength, which is built on prior assessments of selectional preference, identifies the modular semantic structure of predication even when low frequency predications are included. This may be because low-frequency predications are more likely to inscribe novel, loose or figurative associations that reach between semantic clusters to inappropriately decrease the overall modularity if not down-weighted. As a result, more systematic comparison of weighted and unweighted networks, and the relative location of predication within these structures, will reveal where semantic innovation and figurative assertions are most likely to occur. The predication networks analyzed rely on a relatively tight definition of predication, one that, in other languages, may not be accessible by the copular form. Additionally, the two literal interpretations of linguistic predications, equivalence or category membership, may also not be common in all languages. To the extent that parsers or taggers are available, a comparative analysis would broaden the understanding of predication in general.

Given their high modularity, predication structures could be exploited further for a number of NLP tasks. The correlations between centrality and hypernym depth mean that predication networks could help construct or update categorical taxonomies. For example, these networks could help automate the construction of a hypernym taxonomy with weighted branches, potentially augmenting resources like WordNet (Ruiz-Casado et al., 2005; Miller, 1995). One could also examine the growth, combination and bifurcation of specific communities to help track ontological commitments, either over time as shifts in language structures (Gerow and Ahmad, 2012), or across genre and domain (Davies, 2010). Further, because predication encodes categorical information, its community structure may also encode higher-level relations where strong inter-community links imply relationships between classes of objects.

Our study examined the topographical structure of English predications in general, structure that consists, in large part, of hypernym relations. Though the relations in the examined networks are defined by copular `is-a` predication structure, within-community hierarchies correlated only moderately with the hypernym hierarchy in WordNet. This implies that the predications comprising our networks are either not entirely hypernymic or that WordNet is not a good baseline. Indeed, predication is a grammatical relationship that often asserts synonymy or figurative hypernymy (perhaps sometimes also metonymy) and it is not apparent from the surface structure how these semantic interpretation could be disambiguated. One reason this correlation is not higher is likely to do with the low coverage of the copular form as evidence of hypernymy (Hearst, 1992).

Further work regarding the structure of predications could build on the network framework to evaluate the communities themselves. What properties differentiate communities? Are there semantic, lexical or statistical properties that contribute to the formation of communities? Are there discernible differences between words that typify communities as opposed to those that bridge communities? Predication communities are primarily semantic in nature, implying that central nodes would typify meaningful aspects of their community. It would also be relatively easy to extend network representations to address more qualitative aspects such as coherence, word norms and word associations. Indeed, a variety of corpus-based research could employ network-based methods like those exemplified in this paper, capitalizing on graph-theory, social network analysis and statistical physics, without departing from relational structures inherent to language.

Acknowledgments

This work was supported by a grant from the Templeton Foundation to the Metaknowledge Research Network and grant #1158803 from the National Science Foundation.

References

Eneko Agirre, Oier Lpez de Lacalle, and Aitor Soroa. 2014. Random walks for knowledge-based word sense disambiguation. *Computational Linguistics*, 40(1):57–84.

Chris Biemann, Monojit Choudhury, and Animesh Mukherjee. 2009. Syntax is from mars while semantics from venus!: insights from spectral analysis of distributional similarity networks. In *Proceedings of the ACL-IJCNLP 2009 Conference Short Papers*, pages 245–248.

Chris Biemann. 2006. Chinese whispers: an efficient graph clustering algorithm and its application to natural language processing problems. In *Proceedings of the first workshop on graph based methods for natural language processing*, pages 73–80.

Brian F. Bowdle and Dedre Gentner. 2005. The career of metaphor. *Psychological Review*, 112(1):193.

Sharon A. Caraballo. 1999. Automatic construction of a hypernym-labeled noun hierarchy from text. In *Proceedings of the 37th annual meeting of the Association for Computational Linguistics on Computational Linguistics*, pages 120–126.

Philipp Cimiano and Johanna Völker. 2005. Text2onto. In *Natural language processing and information systems*, pages 227–238. Springer.

Philipp Cimiano. 2006. *Ontology learning from text*. Springer.

Aaron M. Cohen, William R. Hersh, Christopher Dubay, and K. Spackman. 2005. Using co-occurrence network structure to extract synonymous gene and protein names from medline abstracts. *BMC Bioinformatics*, 6(1):103.

Mark Davies. 2010. The corpus of contemporary american english as the first reliable monitor corpus of english. *Literary and linguistic computing*, 25(4):447–464.

Günes Erkan and Dragomir R Radev. 2004. Lexrank: Graph-based lexical centrality as salience in text summarization. *Journal of Artificial Intelligence Research*, 22(1):457–479.

Ramon Ferrer i Cancho, Ricard V Solé, and Reinhard Köhler. 2004. Patterns in syntactic dependency networks. *Physical Review E*, 69(5):051915.

Ramon Ferrer i Cancho, Andrea Capocci, and Guido Caldarelli. 2007. Spectral methods cluster words of the same class in a syntactic dependency network. *International Journal of Bifurcation and Chaos*, 17(07):2453–2463.

Peter W. Foltz, Darrell Laham, and Thomas K. Landauer. 1999. Automated essay scoring: Applications to educational technology. In *World Conference on Educational Multimedia, Hypermedia and Telecommunications*, pages 939–944.

Santo Fortunato. 2010. Community detection in graphs. *Physics Reports*, 486(3):75–174.

Dipl-Math Bettina Friedl, Julia Heidemann, et al. 2010. A critical review of centrality measures in social networks. *Business & Information Systems Engineering*, 2(6):371–385.

Aaron Gerow and Khurshid Ahmad. 2012. Diachronic variation in grammatical relationships. In *Proceedings of the 24th International Conference on Computational Linguistics (COLING 2012)*.

Aaron Gerow. 2014. Extracting clusters of specialist terms from unstructured text. In *Proceedings of 2014 Conference on Empirical Methods in Natural Language Processing (forthcoming)*.

Sam Glucksberg, Matthew S. McGlone, and Deanna Manfredi. 1997. Property attribution in metaphor comprehension. *Journal of memory and language*, 36(1):50–67.

Maria Grineva, Maxim Grinev, and Dmitry Lizorkin. 2009. Extracting key terms from noisy and multi-theme documents. In *Proceedings of the 18th international conference on World wide web*, pages 661–670.

Marti A Hearst. 1992. Automatic acquisition of hyponyms from large text corpora. In *Proceedings of the 14th conference on computational linguistics-Volume 2*, pages 539–545.

Adam Kilgarriff, Pavel Rychl, Pavel Smr, and David Tugwell. 2004. The sketch engine. In *Proceedings of EURALEX 2004*, pages 105–116.

Andrea Lancichinetti and Santo Fortunato. 2009. Community detection algorithms: a comparative analysis. *Physical Review E*, 80(5):056117.

Thomas K. Landauer and Susan T. Dumais. 1997. A solution to plato's problem: The latent semantic analysis theory of acquisition, induction, and representation of knowledge. *Psychological Review*, 104(2):211.

Geoffrey Leech, Paul Rayson, and Andrew Wilson. 2001. *Word frequencies in written and spoken English: based on the British National Corpus*. Longman.

George A. Miller. 1995. Wordnet: a lexical database for english. *Communications of the ACM*, 38(11):39–41.

Mark E. J. Newman and M. Girvan. 2004. Finding and evaluating community structure in networks. *Physical Review E*, 69(2):026113.

Mark E. J. Newman. 2010. *Networks: an introduction*. Oxford University Press.

Pascal Pons and Matthieu Latapy. 2005. Computing communities in large networks using random walks. In *Computer and Information Sciences-ISCIS 2005*, pages 284–293. Springer.

Anatol Rapoport, Amnon Rapoport, William P Livant, and John Boyd. 1966. A study of lexical graphs. *Foundations of Language*, pages 338–376.

Philip Resnik. 1997. Selectional preference and sense disambiguation. In *Proceedings of the ACL SIGLEX Workshop on Tagging Text with Lexical Semantics: Why, What, and How*, pages 52–57.

Martin Rosvall and Carl T. Bergstrom. 2008. Maps of random walks on complex networks reveal community structure. *Proceedings of the National Academy of Sciences*, 105(4):1118–1123.

Martin Rosvall and Carl T. Bergstrom. 2011. Multilevel compression of random walks on networks reveals hierarchical organization in large integrated systems. *PloS one*, 6(4):e18209.

Maria Ruiz-Casado, Enrique Alfonseca, and Pablo Castells. 2005. Automatic extraction of semantic relationships for wordnet by means of pattern learning from wikipedia. In *Natural Language Processing and Information Systems*, pages 67–79. Springer.

Ekaterina Shutova, Simone Teufel, and Anna Korhonen. 2013. Statistical metaphor processing. *Computational Linguistics*, 39(2):301–353.

Mark Steyvers and Joshua B. Tenenbaum. 2005. The large-scale structure of semantic networks: Statistical analyses and a model of semantic growth. *Cognitive Science*, 29(1):41–78.

Lin Sun and Anna Korhonen. 2009. Improving verb clustering with automatically acquired selectional preferences. In *Proceedings of the 2009 Conference on Empirical Methods in Natural Language Processing: Volume 2-Volume 2*, pages 638–647.

Peter D. Turney, Patrick Pantel, et al. 2010. From frequency to meaning: Vector space models of semantics. *Journal of Artificial Intelligence Research*, 37(1):141–188.

Jean Véronis. 2004. Hyperlex: lexical cartography for information retrieval. *Computer Speech & Language*, 18(3):223–252.

Yorick Wilks. 1975. A preferential, pattern-seeking, semantics for natural language inference. *Artificial Intelligence*, 6(1):53–74.

Yorick Wilks. 1978. Making preferences more active. *Artificial Intelligence*, 11(3):197–223.

From Visualisation to Hypothesis Construction for Second Language Acquisition

Shervin Malmasi
Centre for Language Technology
Macquarie University
Sydney, NSW, Australia
shervin.malmasi@mq.edu.au

Mark Dras
Centre for Language Technology
Macquarie University
Sydney, NSW, Australia
mark.dras@mq.edu.au

Abstract

One research goal in Second Language Acquisition (SLA) is to formulate and test hypotheses about errors and the environments in which they are made, a process which often involves substantial effort; large amounts of data and computational visualisation techniques promise help here. In this paper we have defined a new task for finding contexts for errors that vary with the native language of the speaker that are potentially useful for SLA research. We propose four models for approaching this task, and find that one based only on error-feature cooccurrence and another based on determining maximum weight cliques in a feature association graph discover strongly distinguishing contexts, with an apparent trade-off between false positives and very specific contexts.

1 Introduction

SLA researchers are interested in a wide variety of aspects of humans learning a new language (L2) different from their native one (L1): cognitive issues and developmental sequences for learners Pienemann (2005), sociocultural factors (Lantolf, 2001), and so on. One long-standing question, dating back to at least Lado (1957), is expressed by Ortega (2009) in the following way: "What is the role played by first language in L2 development, *vis-à-vis* the role of other universal development forces?"

An example of SLA research that looks at this question is the study of Diéz-Bedmar and Papp (2008), comparing Chinese and Spanish learners of English with respect to the English article system (*a*, *an*, *the*) using corpora of essays by native and non-native speakers of English (Granger, 2011). Drawing on the 175 non-native texts, they take a particular theoretical analysis (the so-called Bickerton semantic wheel), use the simple Wordsmith tools designed to extract data for lexicographers to identify errors in a semi-automatic way, and evaluate whether Chinese and Spanish L1 speakers do behave differently via hypothesis testing (ANOVA, chi-square and z-tests, in their case). They conclude that Chinese and Spanish do have characteristic differences, with patterns of zero article and definite article use differing according to semantic context. Such studies are typically carried out on relatively small datasets, and use fairly elementary tools. Sources such as Ellis (2008) and Ortega (2009) give good overviews of such studies and of SLA research in general.

A goal of this paper is to investigate a particular way in which Natural Language Processing (NLP) can usefully contribute to SLA. In terms of existing work, the subfield of Native Language Identification (NLI) has been quite active recently, which looks at predicting the L1 of writers writing in a common L2 within a classification task framework; see for example the recent NLI shared task with 29 entrants (Tetreault et al., 2013).[1] From within linguistics, there has been much interest in how data-driven approaches can contribute to SLA. Granger (2011) discusses a body of work based on the the methodology of carrying out corpus-based approaches to SLA with a focus on NLP tools; Jarvis and Crossley (2012) in an edited collection present recent work by linguists who extend the corpus-based setup by using a text classification approach, looking at what feature selection might say for SLA. From within NLP, Swanson and Charniak (2013) and Swanson and Charniak (2014) take a data-driven approach to SLA investigations much in the spirit of this work.

One particular approach to finding aspects of texts characteristic of their L1s that has motivated the present work is described in Yannakoudakis et al. (2012), the goal of which is to develop visualisation tools for SLA researchers. They present graphs of the relationships between errors and their contexts, such that SLA researchers can navigate through the graphs to find contexts for particular errors that can lead to hypotheses like that of Diéz-Bedmar and Papp (2008) above. In this paper, we look at approaches to finding such hypothesis candidates automatically in the context of L1–L2 interaction by analysing the graphs used in the visualisations

[1] http://sites.google.com/site/nlisharedtask2013/

of Yannakoudakis et al. (2012). Specifically, we do the following:

- We propose a new task that is more directly oriented to SLA research than NLI has been for the most part, with the goal of identifying error-related contexts that are characteristic of L1s.
- We evaluate a number of models for finding such contexts, ranging from a simple baseline to treating the problem as a graph-theoretic maximum weighted clique one.
- We examine the results of some of the models to see how the task and the models might contribute to SLA research.

Because we draw heavily on the work of Yannakoudakis et al. (2012), we first review relevant aspects of that work in §2; we then present our task definition and experimental setup in §3; we give results along with a discussion in §4; we follow with some more detail on related work in §5; and we conclude in §6.

2 Developing Hypotheses: A Visualisation Tool

The context of the Yannakoudakis et al. (2012) work is automated grading of English as a Second or Other Language (ESOL) exam scripts, as described in Briscoe et al. (2010). The automated grading takes a classification approach, using a binary discriminative learner, with useful features including lexical and part-of-speech (PoS) n-grams.

The publicly available dataset on which the work was carried out consists of texts from the First Certificate in English (FCE) exam, aimed at upper-intermediate students of English across various L1s, and was presented in Yannakoudakis et al. (2011). This FCE corpus[2] consists of a subset of 1244 texts of the Cambridge Learner Corpus,[3] and is manually annotated with errors and their corrections, as well as a classification according to an error typology, as in Figure 1.

Yannakoudakis et al. (2012) present their English Profile (EP) visualiser as a way to "visually analyse as well as perform a linguistic interpretation of discriminative features that characterise learner English", using the features of this essay classification task. They define a measure of co-occurrence of features, among themselves and with errors, as a core part of their analysis. Given the set of all sentences in the corpus $S = \{s_1, s_2, \ldots, s_{|S|}\}$ and the set of all features $F = \{f_1, f_2, \ldots, f_{|F|}\}$, a feature $f_i \in F$ is associated with a feature $f_j \in F$ $(i \neq j, 1 \leq i, j \leq M)$ according to the score given in Equation (1), for $s_k \in S, 1 \leq k \leq N$ and $\text{exists}()$ a binary function returning true if the input feature occurs in s_k.

$$\text{score}_{\text{ff}}(f_j, f_i) = \frac{\sum_{k=1}^{|S|} \text{exists}(f_j, f_i, s_k)}{\sum_{k=1}^{|S|} \text{exists}(f_i, s_k)} \quad (1)$$

They mention an analogous measure for feature-error co-occurrence; we assume given the set of all errors $E = \{e_1, e_2, \ldots, e_{|E|}\}$ that this is defined as follows:

$$\text{score}_{\text{ef}}(f_j, e_i) = \frac{\sum_{k=1}^{|S|} \text{exists}(f_j, e_i, s_k)}{\sum_{k=1}^{|S|} \text{exists}(e_i, s_k)} \quad (2)$$

A graph is defined with features and errors as vertices; an edge between features (resp. features and errors) is established if $\text{score}_{\text{ff}}()$ (resp. score_{ef}) is within some user-defined range. This graph of feature–feature (resp. feature–error) relationships is then presented visually.

The paper then presents a case study of how the EP visualiser can be used to assist SLA researchers. The case study starts by noting that RG_JJ_NN1 is the 18th most discriminative negative feature from the essay classifier; then, further inspecting the graph of discriminative features, that it's linked to JJ_NN1_II and VBZ_RG. Then, looking at feature-error relations, it investigates an association with error MD (missing determiner), and presents some examples that match the features (e.g. *Unix is very powerful system but there is one thing against it*), along with a discussion of relationships to various L1s. It is this process of finding interesting features and linking them to particular errors and L1s that we present an approach to automating in this paper.

3 Task Definition & Experimental Setup

At a general level, our goal is to find which kinds of constructions (in a loose sense) centred around errors are particularly characteristic of various L1s.

The specific task we define for this paper, then, is to select a set of features (in the terminology of Yannakoudakis et al. (2012))—which we refer to as the ERROR CONTEXT—that, when combined with the error, show a strong association with L1, in a manner we describe below. So, for example, this may involve finding that an MD error in the context of RG_JJ_NN1, JJ_NN1_II and VBZ_RG shows a strong association with L1. We investigate a number of models for this selection process: the task then is the identification of which models produce poor error contexts (which will not rank highly in hypothesis testing) and which produce good ones (potentially worth considering by an SLA researcher). Below we discuss the data we use, the measure of association for an error and its context, the set of errors chosen, and the models for selecting context.

3.1 Data

The corpus we use for evaluating the models for our task is derived from the FCE corpus of Yannakoudakis et al.

[2] http://ilexir.co.uk/applications/ep-visualiser/

[3] http://www.cup.cam.ac.uk/gb/elt/catalogue/subject/custom/item364603/

Verb Agreement	`<p>Some people <ns type="AGV"><i>says</i><c>say</c></ns> ...</p>`
Incorrect Verb Inflection	`<p>The day I <ns type="IV"><i>shaked</i><c>shook</c></ns> their hands, ...</p>`
Missing Determiner	`<p>I am <ns type="MD"><c>a</c></ns> really good singer.</p>`

Figure 1: FCE corpus examples. Error types indicated by <ns type>...</ns>; errors indicated by <i>...</i>; corrections indicated by <c>...</c>.

language	size
Chinese CHI	66
French FRE	146
German GER	69
Italian ITA	76
Japanese JAP	81
Korean KOR	86
Spanish SPA	200
Turkish TUR	75

Table 1: FCEsub, broken down by language

language	mean
CHI	0.885790
FRE	0.460894
GER	0.366587
ITA	0.581401
JAP	1.058159
KOR	1.067211
SPA	0.472253
TUR	1.014129
F-stat	18.031
sig.	<0.001

Table 2: ANOVA results giving mean score (number of sentences with MD error per 10 sentences) for each language, the ANOVA F-statistic, and significance value

(2012). The full FCE corpus consists of 1244 scripts over 16 languages; script counts range from 2 (Dutch) to 200 (Spanish).

The features used by Yannakoudakis et al. (2012) were derived from their essay classification task. As we are interested in associations with L1, we instead use features from a system submitted to the NLI shared task (Anonymous, 2013), which was applied to a dataset of Test of English as a Foreign Language (TOEFL) scripts: the task and its designated corpus are described in the task overview paper (Tetreault et al., 2013). In this work we use a system trained on the TOEFL11 corpus consisting of texts written in English from speakers of 11 different L1s, with 1100 essays per L1 and balanced across topic. We only use PoS n-grams ($n = 1, 2, 3$) as features in this work. Note that we use the terminology of Yannakoudakis et al. (2012) here: what had their origin as features in the essay classification task are still referred to as features in the visualisation tool, although the task carried out there is not a classification one. Similarly, we refer to our PoS n-grams as features, although we are not classifying errors using these features and so are not carrying out feature selection for the typical purpose of optimising classification performance.

For this, as did Yannakoudakis et al. (2012), we use the RASP parser (Briscoe et al., 2006) for tagging; the tags are consequently from the CLAWS2 tagset,[4] which are more fine-grained in terms of linguistic analysis than the more frequently used Penn Treebank tags.

For our task, we then used the subset of the FCE corpus where the languages overlapped with the TOEFL11 corpus: we refer to this as FCEsub. This gives 799 scripts over 8 languages, distributed as in Table 1; a positive byproduct is that the L1s are more similar in size than the full FCE corpus.

[4]http://ucrel.lancs.ac.uk/claws2tags.html

3.2 Association Measure

We noted in §1 that SLA studies such as Diéz-Bedmar and Papp (2008) use standard hypothesis testing techniques. We take this as a starting point. We could, for example, evaluate whether a particular raw error (that is, without a feature context) is strongly associated with L1s by using a single factor ANOVA test.[5] The independent variable would be the L1. The dependent variable could be one of a number of alternatives; we choose the number of sentences with a particular error per 10 sentences.[6] To illustrate, we give the ANOVA results from FCEsub for the MD error in Table 2. The ANOVA calculation is based on an F-statistic which compares variance between treatments against variance within treatments; this is compared against critical values for the F-statistic to determine statistical significance. The expected value of the F-statistic under the null hypothesis is 1, with values above 1 increasingly inconsistent with the null hypothesis. The data in Table 2 shows that the MD error does vary significantly with L1; a post-hoc Tukey HSD test lets us identify which specific languages exhibit this difference and shows that, for example (and as can be observed in the means), German L1 speakers are significantly different from Korean L1 speakers in the occurrence of MD errors.

For our task we are not interested in significance per se. Rather, we are interested in whether we can find occurrences of errors plus contexts that are more strongly associated with, or that vary across, L1s, e.g. that an

[5]See, e.g., Jackson (2009).

[6]We note that the texts differ significantly in length by L1, so it would not be suitable to normalise as occurrences per document.

type	name	F-stat	p-val	N
DJ	Wrong Derived Adjective	3.27	.002	332
DN	Wrong Derived Noun	0.70	.671	294
MD	Missing Determiner	18.03	.000	1702
MT	Missing Preposition	2.81	.007	985
UD	Unnecessary Determiner	1.20	.301	807
UT	Unnecessary Preposition	0.26	.968	689
UV	Unnecessary Verb	0.78	.606	317

Table 3: Error types chosen for evaluation, including F-statistic, ANOVA p-value and corpus count of sentences containing error.

MD error in the context of `RG_JJ_NN1`, `JJ_NN1_II` and `VBZ_RG` is more strongly associated with L1s; and we are also interested in which of our proposed methods for identifying an error's feature context does this best. For this purpose, then, we use just the F-statistic from the ANOVA test, this time with the dependent variable as the ratio of occurrences of error plus error context per 10 sentences: a higher F-statistic shows a stronger association with L1s.[7]

We also consider the χ^2-statistic from Pearson's chi-squared test, noting that it is also used in SLA hypothesis testing and that it was additionally found by Swanson and Charniak (2013) to be good at distinguishing interesting features in their related task (see §5 for more detail). The F-statistic and χ^2-statistic are closely related: a random variate of the F-distribution is the ratio of two chi-squared variates scaled by their degrees of freedom. A difference is that χ^2 compares observed versus expected counts rather than proportions: to take account of the differing text lengths, our observed frequency is the number of sentences with error and error context per L1; our expected frequency is the total number of sentences with that error and error context scaled according to the proportion of sentences labelled with that L1 relative to the corpus as a whole.

3.3 Errors Chosen

From the 74 error types in the FCE corpus, we select a subset to evaluate our models. In addition to the MD error used in the case study of Yannakoudakis et al. (2012), we choose a subset which has a range of F-statistic values as described above: some show very similar patterns across L1s (i.e. with low F-statistic), such as DN Wrong Derived Noun (e.g. *hot* vs *heat*); others do vary significantly with L1, such as DJ Wrong Derived Adjective (e.g. *reasonally* vs *reasonable*). Having errors with a range of F-statistic values lets us evaluate whether finding good error contexts works only for strongly L1-associated errors, weakly L1-associated errors, or across the spectrum. Our subset is in Table 3, along with their F-statistic, ANOVA p-value and counts in FCESUB.

3.4 Models

We propose four models for choosing error contexts. These models rank error contexts; we evaluate the ranked error contexts by F-statistic and χ^2-statistic values (§3.2).

ERRORCOOCC In this model we rank features by error-feature co-occurrence scores given by Equation (2). The L1 is not taken into account, so this will just return common features which may be equally strongly associated with errors across all L1s. We look at results for when $k = 1..3$ features are chosen. For $k = 2, 3$, we add the individual error-feature scores together for the ranking.[8] It may be the case that interesting results could be obtained for $k > 3$, but we only look at the $k = 1..3$ in this preliminary work to see if there are any discernible trends suggesting that larger values of k could help.

L1ASSOC Here we use features that are strongly associated with the L1s from the TOEFL11 corpus and NLI shared task. Specifically, we rank features by their Information Gain with respect to L1s as in the process of feature selection from the shared task.[9] The relationship between errors and features (in the form of error-feature co-occurrence scores) is not taken into account here. Again, we look at results for when $k = 1..3$ features are chosen, and for $k = 2, 3$, we add the individual error-feature scores together for the ranking.

MAXWEIGHTCLIQUE Both of the preceding models look only at one factor that might be relevant: error-feature scores (finding features that are related to the errors) and a measure of the association of features with L1s; but there is no link between them, and interaction of features is not taken into account. In Yannakoudakis et al. (2012), the visualiser provides to the SLA researcher a graph showing the relatedness of features, based on Equation (1), and the SLA researcher combines this with error-feature scores to find interesting candidate error contexts; we create a similar graph and aim to imitate the process by incorporating error-feature scores as follows.

We define a weighted undirected graph $G = (V, A)$ such that V is the set of features used in the above models (i.e. PoS n-grams from ERRORCOOCC); A is defined such that $(v_i, v_j) \in A$ for vertices $v_i, v_j \in V$ if $0.8 \leq \text{score}_{\text{ff}}(v_i, v_j) \leq 1.0$ where $\text{score}_{\text{ff}}()$ is as defined as in Equation (1).[10] Given our set of errors E defined at Equation (2) above, the weight of a vertex v_i is defined as $\text{score}_{\text{ef}}(v_i, e_j)$ for some $e_j \in E$.

[7]As we are only using the F-statistic to evaluate ranks, we do not need a multiple comparison adjustment such as the Bonferroni correction: this would only apply for comparisons to a significance threshold, and in any case the Bonferroni is monotonic and does not affect rankings.

[8]For $k = 2$ the combinations were made from the top 100 features from $k = 1$, and for $k = 3$ from the top 50.

[9]We recalculated this over the subset of eight languages used in this paper.

[10]We choose this threshold value as it is the one used in the graph definition of Yannakoudakis et al. (2012).

model	r
ErrorCoocc	0.95
L1Assoc	0.97
MaxWeightClique	0.95
MaxWeightClique-L1	0.92

Table 4: Average correlation coefficient r between F-statistic and χ^2-statistic for each model

Given this graph, it is possible to characterise the finding of related features with strong aggregate associations with errors as an instance of the MAXIMUM WEIGHT CLIQUE PROBLEM (Bomze et al., 1999). As the name suggests, this finds a clique of maximum weight, here the strongest aggregate feature–error association. While this is an NP-hard problem, there are quite efficient algorithms for solving it; we use one proposed by Östergård (1999).[11]

MaxWeightClique-L1 We also look at a variant of MaxWeightClique where we construct the graphs based only on relationships among features for a particular L1. That is, there will be eight weighted graphs per error of interest.

4 Results and Discussion

4.1 Overall Results

We only present the F-statistic results here; the χ^2-statistic showed very similar patterns. The average correlation between the two for each model shows the strong similarity (Table 4).

For the F-statistic results, presented in Table 5, we report the highest F-statistic in the N-best list ($N = 1, 5, 20, 50$) for each model. For models ErrorCoocc and L1Assoc we report the highest F-statistic for each value of k ($k = 1, 2, 3$). The number of occurrences of the error context with the highest F-statistic is given in parentheses after the F-statistic; the highest value for each N is in bold. For MaxWeightClique-L1, we also note the language of the graph from which the highest score was derived.

We note by comparing Table 5 with Table 3 that for each error type except for MD, it is possible to find an error context that is more strongly associated with L1s than is the raw error type alone. For MD this is not surprising, as its frequency of occurrence is very strongly linked to the L1, as noted in Table 2 and §3.2.[12] (For the error type MT also, no model produces an error context more strongly associated with the L1 for the single best choice where $N = 1$, but does for larger values of N.)

[11]Code for the used *wclique* is available at `http://tcs.legacy.ics.tkk.fi/~pat/wclique.html`.

[12]The fact that determiner errors are very widely studied in terms of analysing cross-linguistic influence suggests a broad consensus that they vary strongly with L1. In addition to Diéz-Bedmar and Papp (2008), a sample of other studies includes Parrish (1987), Young (1996) and Ionin and Montrul (2010).

With respect to the individual models, the simple ErrorCoocc scores highly, giving the best result about half the time, and the best results can occur for any of $k = 1, 2, 3$. The number of instances returned for each error plus error context is larger than for the other models as well, which is not surprising as the model aims to find contexts strongly associated with the errors rather than with L1s. However, these are then likely to be features that are fairly common across L1s; we look at some examples in §4.2.

L1Assoc performs fairly poorly on our evaluation measure, although in many cases it does find an error context more strongly associated with the L1 than just the raw error type. Counts are also lower. Also, for this model, $k = 2, 3$ are always worse than $k = 1$: bringing in a second context feature reduces the number of occurrences to such an extent that the F-statistic can drop dramatically. This is probably in part an artefact of the size of the FCE corpus (and particularly our FCEsub subcorpus): these features derived from the TOEFL11 corpus just do not occur sufficiently often in our evaluation corpus (and in fact there are often large numbers of zero occurrences for $k = 2, 3$).

MaxWeightClique also performs fairly poorly. However, in many cases it also finds an error context more strongly associated with L1 than the raw error type alone (DN, MT, UD, UT, UV), even if not always for $N = 1$, and it has intermediate counts of occurrences.

MaxWeightClique-L1 gives the best results in the other half of the cases where ErrorCoocc does not. The error contexts that it finds, however, are very specific, often to a single language (as might be expected by its definition) with very small numbers of counts.

4.2 Some Examples

We look at some examples in Figure 2, to illustrate both interesting error contexts found and areas where the models do a poor job. In these sample sentences, only errors of interest are retained and highlighted.

The DJ error with context { `JJ`, `NN1` } illustrates the top result found under the ErrorCoocc model for $N = 20$. In the first sentence the model seems to find a useful pattern: the adjective that is at the centre of the error occurs in the context of a singular noun. On the other hand, the second sentence illustrates a problem: because the range of the context is the whole sentence, frequent features such as `NN1` will occur a lot in other parts of the sentence that have no apparent relation to the actual error. The ErrorCoocc model is thus likely to be picking up false positives by virtue of the relatively high frequencies of its error contexts.

The UV error with context { `TO_VV0_II`, `NNL1`, `II`, `NN2`, `VV0_II` } illustrates the top result found under the MaxWeightClique-L1 model for $N = 5$. This is very specific, and its three instances only appear in Turkish. But all three are similar errors from different documents, so it appears likely to be a genuine pattern, although the `NN2` seems only to have a tenuous

error	N	ErrorCoocc	L1Assoc	MaxWeightClique	MaxWeightClique-L1
DJ	1	2.78(274) / **3.19**(227) / 2.95(158)	1.59(31) / 1.59(31) / 0.81(6)	0.99(15)	3.08(2) [GER]
	5	**3.60**(268) / 3.19(227) / 3.02(148)	2.19(12) / 1.59(31) / 0.81(6)	1.74(41)	3.24(2) [CHI]
	20	3.72(194) / 3.33(163) / **4.02**(93)	2.53(70) / 1.59(31) / 1.36(1)	2.34(24)	3.50(5) [ITA]
	50	3.72(194) / 3.39(114) / **4.02**(93)	2.58(107) / 1.59(31) / 1.59(31)	2.48(18)	3.84(3) [ITA]
DN	1	0.77(268) / 1.63(185) / 1.73(119)	1.09(40) / 1.09(40) / 0.70(7)	1.26(63)	**3.24**(2) [CHI]
	5	1.80(191) / 2.29(153) / 2.54(142)	1.25(5) / 1.36(1) / 1.36(1)	1.26(63)	**3.24**(2) [CHI]
	20	2.34(86) / 2.69(144) / 2.95(113)	2.04(26) / 1.36(1) / 1.36(1)	1.76(30)	**3.24**(2) [CHI]
	50	2.86(61) / 3.16(120) / 2.95(113)	3.89(4) / 2.75(2) / 2.75(2)	3.41(18)	**4.27**(10) [SPA]
MD	1	**14.28**(1319) / 9.09(985) / 6.38(753)	5.83(198) / 5.83(198) / 0.54(2)	3.07(297)	4.05(91) [KOR]
	5	**14.28**(1310) / 12.18(769) / 6.75(582)	8.20(268) / 5.83(198) / 1.93(3)	5.83(198)	5.83(198) [KOR]
	20	**14.41**(850) / 12.18(769) / 6.82(593)	8.20(268) / 5.83(198) / 2.60(36)	5.83(198)	5.83(198) [KOR]
	50	**14.41**(850) / 12.18(769) / 7.99(483)	8.36(831) / 5.83(198) / 5.83(198)	5.83(198)	6.47(110) [KOR]
MT	1	**3.34**(794) / 3.00(666) / 3.02(485)	1.85(79) / 1.85(79) / 1.55(13)	1.70(61)	2.48(20) [CHI]
	5	3.34(794) / 3.46(478) / 3.37(378)	2.54(101) / 1.85(79) / 1.55(13)	2.14(64)	**4.47**(3) [CHI]
	20	4.44(295) / 3.64(375) / **4.60**(294)	4.44(295) / 3.11(25) / 3.11(25)	2.79(44)	4.47(3) [CHI]
	50	4.50(277) / **5.21**(247) / 4.72(215)	4.44(295) / 3.86(33) / 3.11(25)	4.54(74)	4.61(3) [GER]
UD	1	0.69(679) / 1.05(475) / **2.08**(334)	1.45(62) / 1.45(62) / 0.73(10)	0.64(47)	1.54(20) [GER]
	5	1.70(405) / 1.17(452) / 2.08(334)	1.59(26) / 1.45(62) / 1.36(1)	1.45(62)	**3.54**(9) [CHI]
	20	2.08(223) / 2.11(360) / 2.32(276)	3.41(51) / 1.45(62) / 1.36(1)	1.90(29)	**3.93**(3) [ITA]
	50	3.27(112) / 3.01(188) / 2.33(198)	3.41(51) / 1.54(4) / 1.54(4)	2.85(66)	**4.06**(3) [ITA]
UT	1	0.14(548) / 0.45(414) / 1.12(259)	1.01(51) / 1.01(51) / 0.43(1)	0.81(35)	**3.06**(2) [GER]
	5	0.82(368) / 1.16(321) / 1.58(249)	2.28(23) / 1.36(1) / 1.36(1)	1.01(51)	**4.10**(3) [TUR]
	20	1.51(351) / 1.77(275) / 1.89(225)	2.91(51) / 1.53(6) / 1.36(1)	2.58(45)	**4.10**(3) [TUR]
	50	2.25(112) / 2.66(201) / 3.18(178)	2.91(51) / 1.53(6) / 1.36(1)	2.58(45)	**4.10**(3) [TUR]
UV	1	0.88(260) / 0.97(186) / 1.18(119)	1.06(15) / 1.06(15) / 1.29(2)	1.49(28)	**2.53**(2) [JAP]
	5	2.22(175) / 2.21(162) / 1.68(109)	2.29(8) / 1.29(2) / 1.29(2)	1.49(28)	**4.09**(3) [TUR]
	20	2.25(125) / 2.82(127) / 3.13(96)	3.22(8) / 1.52(1) / 1.52(1)	2.38(15)	**4.09**(3) [TUR]
	50	2.56(61) / 3.01(101) / 3.13(96)	3.22(8) / 1.52(1) / 1.52(1)	2.38(15)	**4.63**(3) [CHI]

Table 5: Results for the chosen error types under the four proposed models. All error types and models report the best F-statistic for the selected error context and frequency within the top N ($N = 1, 5, 20, 50$). ErrorCoocc and L1Assoc give the best score for the set of k features ($k = 1, 2, 3$). MaxWeightClique-L1 also notes the language graph with the best result.

error	context	example sentences
DJ	JJ, NN1	Basically/RR ,/, I/PPIS1 helped/VVD them/PPHO2 liaise/VV0 with/IW the/AT local/JJ police/NN and/CC get/VV0 some/DD <ns type="DJ"><i>electronical</i><c>**electronic/JJ**</c></ns> **equipment/NN1** that/CST they/PPHS2 needed/VVD.
		The/AT **show/NN1** will/VM be/VB0 at/II the/AT Central/JJ **Exhibition/NN1** Hall/NP1 and/CC it/PPH1 will/VM be/VB0 <ns type="DJ"><i>opened</i><c>**open/JJ**</c></ns> until/ICS 7/MC.
UV	TO_VV0_II, NNL1, II, NN2, VV0_II	I/PPIS1 used/VMK **to/TO** <ns type="UV"><i>be</i></ns> **play/VV0 in/II** the/AT **school/NNL1** team/NN1 ... and/CC our/APP$ team/NN1 was/VBDZ one/MC1 of/IO the/AT best/JJT basketball/NN1 **teams/NN2** ...
DN	XX, XX_VV0, VM_XX_VV0, NN1	Never/RR the/AT less/DAR ,/, in/II summer/NNT1 we/PPIS2 **can/VM n't/XX resist/VV0** such/DA <ns type="DN"><i>hot</i><c>**heat/NN1**</c></ns>!
		... I/PPIS1 think/VV0 you/PPY should/VM have/VH0 a/AT1 <ns type="DN"><i>baby-parking</i><c>kindergarten/NP1</c></ns> ,/, in/II fact/NN1 a/AT1 certain/JJ number/NN1 of/IO women/NN2 **could/VM n't/XX see/VV0** the/AT **Festival/NN1** because/CS of/IO their/APP$ sons/NN2.
MD	VBZ_RG, RG_JJ_NN1	The/AT first/MD and/CC most/RR important/JJ thing/NN1 **is/VBZ that/RG modern/JJ technology/NN1** has/VHZ made/VVN our/APP$ life/NN1 easier/JJR ,/, for/IF instance/NN1 <ns type="MD"><c>the/AT</c></ns> rice/NN1 cooker/NN1 is/VBZ a/AT1 great/JJ invention/NN1 ...

Figure 2: Examples for sample error types and specific error contexts. Error contexts are bolded.

connection.

The DN error with context { XX, XX_VV0, VM_XX_VV0, NN1 } illustrates the top result found under the MAXWEIGHTCLIQUE-L1 model for $N = 50$. A number of this reasonably sized set are similar to the first sentence, where the context appears interesting. In this example, *hot* is used for *heat*; the other examples of this type are from Spanish and Italian (similarly, e.g., *live* for *life*), where the error seems to be connected to words where the English derivational morphology is not simply affixation. However, there are some like the second sentence, where (as for the DJ error) the error context appears in a different clause, and likely irrelevant.

The MD error in the last row we examine because (a more complex version of) it was the focus of the case study in Yannakoudakis et al. (2012), which from the examples of that paper looked quite convincing as an error context of relevance to SLA research. However, it and the related examples of Yannakoudakis et al. (2012) were not in the publicly available corpus,[13] and in fact there is only one example of this error and context in the whole FCE corpus, illustrating the issue of data sparsity. Further, this example also illustrates the issue of tagging error: *that* is tagged as RG (degree adverb) where it should be CST.

So as might be anticipated from the frequency numbers in Table 5, the MAXWEIGHTCLIQUE-L1 model produces context that looks interesting from an SLA perspective, but is relatively limited in scope; the ERROR-COOCC model produces a much larger set of candidates, and can successfully find error context such that they behave differently with respect to the L1s according to the ANOVA F-statistic, but produces false positives. Overall, a recurring issue illustrated for all models by the examples is the proposal of error context far away from any likely relevance to SLA.

5 Related Work

While Native Language Identification (NLI) as a subfield of NLP has seen much new work in the last few years — the papers from the shared task (Tetreault et al., 2013) provide a recent sample — the emphasis on optimising classification task results, for example by using classifier ensembles (Malmasi et al., 2013), versus analysing features for relevance to other tasks has varied. Below we discuss works which directly look at how features might be related to language-learning tasks or SLA research.

The seminal work of Koppel et al. (2005) that presented NLI as a classification task included, in addition to standard lexical and PoS n-gram features, errors made by the writers; these errors were automatically identified using Microsoft Word grammar checker. Kochmar (2011) used the FCE corpus for NLI, including the manually annotated errors as features, and presented an analysis of usefulness of features (including errors) with respect to L1.

Wong and Dras (2011) used syntactic features on the basis of SLA theory that posits that L1 constructions may be reflected in some form of characteristic errors or patterns in L2 constructions to some extent, or through overuse or avoidance of particular constructions in L2 (Lado, 1957; Ellis, 2008); they did note distributional differences of features related to L1. Wong et al. (2012) induced topic models over function words and PoS n-grams, where some of the topics appeared to reflect L1-specific characteristics. These works, while interested in the nature of the features, do not evaluate them except via classification accuracy.

Swanson and Charniak (2012) similarly explore using syntax, where they propose a richer representation

[13]We assume that the multiple examples come from the larger CLC corpus.

for L1-specific constructions through Tree Substitution Grammar (TSG). Swanson and Charniak (2013) subsequently examine both relevancy and redundancy of features through a number of metrics (including the χ^2-statistic used in this paper). They then extend a Bayesian induction model for TSG inference based on a supervised mixture of hierarchical grammars, in order to extract a filtered set of more linguistically informed features that could benefit both NLI and SLA research; an aim was to find relatively rare features that are nevertheless useful for L1 prediction. Swanson and Charniak (2014) continue on from this with a data-driven approach to inferring possible relationships between L1 and L2 structures, again using TSGs. Malmasi and Dras (2014c) also propose a method for identifying potential language transfer effects by using additional linguistic features such as adaptor grammars and grammatical dependencies to analyse differences in learner language. This body of work thus shares some similarities with the present paper, but our focus is on errors rather than on the distributional differences, and we look at error contexts that may not constitute a TSG tree or grammatical dependency.

Coming from a linguistic perspective, the works in Jarvis and Crossley (2012) use Linear Discriminant Analysis for classification of texts by L1, and identify interesting features by a stepwise feature selection process in the course of classification, rather than via the measurement of their variability across L1s as here.

More recently, several of these NLI techniques have been adapted and applied to languages other than English, such as Arabic and Chinese (Malmasi and Dras, 2014a; Malmasi and Dras, 2014b).

6 Conclusion

In this paper, prompted by work on using computational visualisation techniques to help SLA researchers form hypotheses about errors and the environments in which they are made, we have defined a new task for finding interesting contexts for errors that vary with the native language of the speaker. We proposed four models, ranging from one based on simple error-feature co-occurrence statistics to one based on the maximum weighted clique on an L1-specific feature association graph; these all managed to find contexts that were more strongly associated with L1s than the raw errors alone, and produced (albeit with many false positives in the case of the simple model) some error contexts that look potentially useful for SLA.

This paper is largely intended to prompt more work on applying NLP techniques to SLA more broadly. As such, there are many ways in which the work could be further developed. First, to get rid of obviously incorrect cases, the size of the area over which the feature-feature and feature-error scores are calculated could be restricted, perhaps to the relevant clause or a certain window size. Second, it may not be the case that the ANOVA F-statistic or χ^2 are the best evaluation measure: in medical work, for example, there is the notion of clinical significance, which takes effect size into account and is often more relevant to the practitioner than statistical significance. Similarly, the current features may not be the most meaningful. As part of this, an important step would be to bring in SLA researchers, to assess proposed error contexts and look at what evaluation measures best relate to this. The role of the present work would then be to rule out models for producing error contexts (like L1ASSOC) that produce weaker results in hypothesis testing: it would thus be complementary to the visualisation work from which it stems, guiding SLA researchers away from unproductive areas of the space of possible hypotheses. And third, the size of the corpus is (as always) an issue: as these error-annotated corpora are few and far between, a semi-supervised approach or one that in some way incorporated unannotated data would be useful, perhaps using some of the extensive recent work on error annotation.

References

Immanuel M. Bomze, Marco Budinich, Panos Pardalos, and Marcello Pelillo. 1999. The Maximum Clique Problem. In D.-Z. Du and P. M. Pardalos, editors, *Handbook of Combinatorial Optimization (supp. Vol. A)*, pages 1–74. Kluwer Academic, Dordrecht, Netherlands.

Ted Briscoe, John Carroll, and Rebecca Watson. 2006. The second release of the RASP system. In *Proc. of the COLING/ACL Interactive Presentation Sessions*, pages 77–80, Stroudsburg, PA, USA.

Ted Briscoe, Ben Medlock, and Øistein Andersen. 2010. Automated Assessment of ESOL Free Text Examinations. Technical Report TR-790, University of Cambridge, Computer Laboratory.

María Belén Diéz-Bedmar and Szilvia Papp. 2008. The use of the English article system by Chinese and Spanish learners. *Language and Computers*, 66(1):147–176.

Rod Ellis. 2008. *The Study of Second Language Acquisition, 2nd edition.* Oxford University Press, Oxford, UK.

Sylviane Granger. 2011. How to Use Foreign and Second Language Learner Corpora. In Alison Mackey and Susan M. Gass, editors, *Research Methods in Second Language Acquisition: A Practical Guide.* Wiley-Blackwell.

Tania Ionin and Silvina Montrul. 2010. The role of L1 transfer in the interpretation of articles with definite plurals. *Language Learning*, 60(4):877–925.

Sherri L. Jackson. 2009. *Statistics: Plain and Simple.* Wadsworth, Cengage Learning, Belmont, CA, US.

Scott Jarvis and Scott Crossley, editors. 2012. *Approaching Language Transfer Through Text Classification: Explorations in the Detection-based Approach.* Multilingual Matters, Bristol, UK.

Ekaterina Kochmar. 2011. Identification of a writer's native language by error analysis. MPhil thesis, University of Cambridge.

Moshe Koppel, Jonathan Schler, and Kfir Zigdon. 2005. Automatically determining an anonymous author's native language. In *Intelligence and Security Informatics*, volume 3495 of *LNCS*, pages 209–217. Springer-Verlag.

Robert Lado. 1957. *Linguistics Across Cultures: Applied Linguistics for Language Teachers*. Univ. of Michigan Press, Ann Arbor, MI, US.

James P. Lantolf. 2001. *Sociocultural Theory and Second Language Learning*. Oxford University Press, Oxford, UK.

Shervin Malmasi and Mark Dras. 2014a. Arabic Native Language Identification. In *Proceedings of the Arabic Natural Language Processing Workshop (co-located with EMNLP 2014)*, Doha, Qatar, October. Association for Computational Linguistics.

Shervin Malmasi and Mark Dras. 2014b. Chinese Native Language Identification. *Proceedings of the 14th Conference of the European Chapter of the Association for Computational Linguistics*.

Shervin Malmasi and Mark Dras. 2014c. Language Transfer Hypotheses with Linear SVM Weights. *Proceedings of the 2014 Conference on Empirical Methods in Natural Language Processing (EMNLP)*.

Shervin Malmasi, Sze-Meng Jojo Wong, and Mark Dras. 2013. NLI Shared Task 2013: MQ Submission. In *Proceedings of the Eighth Workshop on Innovative Use of NLP for Building Educational Applications*, pages 124–133, Atlanta, Georgia, June. Association for Computational Linguistics.

Lourdes Ortega. 2009. *Understanding Second Language Acquisition*. Hodder Education, Oxford, UK.

Patric Östergård. 1999. A New Algorithm for the Maximum-Weight Clique Problem. *Electronic Notes in Discrete Mathematics*, 3:153–156, May.

Betsy Parrish. 1987. A New Look at Methodologies in the Study of Article Acquisition for Learners of ESL. *Language Learning*, 37(3):361–384.

Manfred Pienemann. 2005. *Cross-linguistic Aspects of Processability Theory*. John Benjamins, Amsterdam, Netherlands.

Benjamin Swanson and Eugene Charniak. 2012. Native Language Detection with Tree Substitution Grammars. In *Proc. Meeting Assoc. Computat. Linguistics (ACL)*, pages 193–197.

Ben Swanson and Eugene Charniak. 2013. Extracting the native language signal for second language acquisition. In *Proc. Conf. North American Assoc. for Computat. Linguistics: Human Language Technologies (NAACL-HLT)*, pages 85–94, Atlanta, Georgia, June.

Ben Swanson and Eugene Charniak. 2014. Data Driven Language Transfer Hypotheses. In *Proc. Conf. European Assoc. for Computat. Linguistics (EACL)*, pages 169–173, Gothenburg, Sweden, April.

Joel Tetreault, Daniel Blanchard, and Aoife Cahill. 2013. A report on the first native language identification shared task. In *Proceedings of the Eighth Workshop on Innovative Use of NLP for Building Educational Applications (BEA)*, pages 48–57, Atlanta, Georgia, June.

Sze-Meng Jojo Wong and Mark Dras. 2011. Exploiting parse structures for native language identification. In *Proc. Conf. Empirical Methods in Natural Language Processing (EMNLP)*, pages 1600–1610.

Sze-Meng Jojo Wong, Mark Dras, and Mark Johnson. 2012. Exploring Adaptor Grammars for Native Language Identification. In *Proc. Conf. Empirical Methods in Natural Language Processing (EMNLP)*, pages 699–709.

Helen Yannakoudakis, Ted Briscoe, and Ben Medlock. 2011. A New Dataset and Method for Automatically Grading ESOL Texts. In *Proc. Meeting Assoc. Computat. Linguistics (ACL)*, pages 180–189.

Helen Yannakoudakis, Ted Briscoe, and Theodora Alexopoulou. 2012. Automating Second Language Acquisition Research: Integrating Information Visualisation and Machine Learning. In *Proc. EACL Workshop of LINGVIS & UNCLH*, pages 35–43.

Richard Young. 1996. Form-Function Relations in Articles in English Interlanguage. In R. Bayley and D. R. Preston, editors, *Second Language Acquisition and Linguistic Variation*, pages 135–175. John Benjamins, Amsterdam, The Netherlands.

Author Index